IN PRAISE OF SLEEP
SELECTED POEMS OF LUCIAN BLAGA

Translated and with an Introduction by

ANDREI CODRESCU

BLACK
WIDOW
PRESS

BOSTON

Black Widow Press is an imprint of Commonwealth Books, Inc., Boston, MA. Distributed to the trade by NBN (National Book Network) throughout North America, Canada, and the U.K. Black Widow Press and its logo are registered trademarks of Commonwealth Books, Inc.

Joseph S. Phillips and Susan J. Wood, Ph.D., Publishers
www.blackwidowpress.com

Cover design & text production: Geoff Munsterman

Cover images: bronze iteration from Constantin Brâncuşi's "Bird in Space" [Pasărea în văzduh] series (c. 1928). Image taken from Solomon R. Guggenheim Museum website: www.guggenheim.org; Romanian stamp of Lucian Blaga (c. 1995).

ISBN-13: 978-0-9995803-6-3

Printed in the United States of America

CONTENTS

THE FOOTPRINTS OF THE PROPHET (1921)

IN THE GREAT PASSING (1924)

IN PRAISE OF SLEEP (1929)

ON THE GREAT WATER DIVIDE (1933)

AT THE COURT OF YEARNING (1938)

THE UNSUSPECTED STAIR (NEW VERSE, 1943)

INTRODUCTION
by Andrei Codrescu

Lucian Blaga's life began and ended in two emblematic silences. Born on May 9, 1895, in the village of Lancrăm in Transylvania, Romania, he did not speak until he was four years old. "My beginnings stand under a fabulous absence of the word.... Not even an awkward fumbling at the edges of sound, not even a sign of articulate speech." His mother tempted him out of his silence during a long night of pleading, and the next day, "I began speaking in full sentences.... Ashamed, I held my hand over my eyes, and spoke. From under the eaves of my fingers and hand, with which I was still defending myself from the world of the word, my voice came whole, drop by drop" (*Chronicle and Song of My Years*).

In 1949, after the Communist takeover of Romania, Lucian Blaga, one of Romania's most distinguished poets, was once more forced into silence. "The Unexpected Stair," his last authentic book of poetry, appeared in 1943. In 1962 he was "rehabilitated," but the poems from shortly before his death on May 6, 1961, as well as his posthumously published work, seem written by someone else, someone who tried to speak from the depths of a great silence with a voice borrowed from a former self. Few of these poems cross the border into the light. Instead they join the great inarticulate world of the mute child.

Blaga's silences form a great parenthesis between which not only his work but the history of modern Romanian poetry are enfolded. The period between the two world wars was Romania's golden age of modernism. Tudor Arghezi, Ion Barbu, Ilarie Voronca, Tristan Tzara, Eugène Ionescu, Mircea Eliade, E.M. Cioran, Paul Celan are some of the names, in addition to Blaga's, which have become more or less familiar in the West. The creative atmosphere in Bucharest, Cluj, and other Romanian cities between the wars was explosive. Twentieth-century ideas descended on our small Balkan country all at once and were quickly absorbed and transformed. A vital, young, and literate nation read, discussed, and incorporated them with astonishing speed.

Before long, original Romanian contributions to European dialogue began to appear. Literary reviews and poetry supplements in newspapers combined with a vigorous cafe life gave Romanians the feeling (temporary, alas!) that they were indeed part of the West.

Transylvania, where Blaga was born, did not become part of Romania until 1919, the same year that Blaga's first book of poetry, *Poems of Light*, appeared, a symbolic event greeted with enthusiasm by Romanian intellectuals on both sides of the Carpathians. Blaga was called the gift of the Romanian spirit to the reunification of the long-separated Romanian provinces.

Until the end of the First World War, Transylvania had been part of the Austro-Hungarian empire, whose official language was German. Blaga received a thoroughly German education. He was enrolled in German primary schools in Sebeş-Alba, then went to the Andrei Şaguna Gymnasium in Braşov, where he began a passionate philosophical romance with Schopenhauer, Hölderin, Lessing, Nietzsche, and especially Henri Bergson, philosophers whose thinking and styles influenced him profoundly. He acquired the "vice of metaphysics" from them: "Metaphysics was becoming more and more my incurable vice, my demonic passion. Beyond all Kantian reservations, I was beginning to appreciate metaphysical works as *creations*, and I came under their thrall with a feeling of sacred drunkenness." *(Chronicle and Song of My Years).*

Blaga's addiction to metaphysics clashed with his upbringing and later with his higher education at the theological seminary in Sibiu, where he enrolled both to escape induction in the imperial army and because his father had been a priest. Romanian Orthodoxy was not real Christianity to Blaga, but rather "ancient paganism dressed in Christian forms," an opinion that did not sit well with his elders. His father, though a simple country priest and a taciturn man, had not rejected the modern world: he had passed a mechanic's test and brought a threshing machine into the village. Blaga's later rejection of all forms of progress and the resolutely antitechnological pantheism of his poetic world were a revolt against his father. There were also the foundation for an original antimaterialist philosophy.

Blaga's early lectures in German philosophy were important to his intellectual development, but he did not conceive of an art equal to his intuitive understanding of philosophical problems until he went to Vienna in the summer of 1916. Here he encountered Expressionist manifestos, poetry, and art. He immediately abandoned his tentative poetic attempts, which had until that time been little more than exercises in the classical Symbolist fashion of the nineteenth century. He recognised in Expressionism an "evident, transparent, axiomatic" body of ideas.

In the same year he met Cornelia Brediceanu, his future wife. She had been educated in Switzerland, and she introduced him to the writings of the new generation of poets writing in French, including Francis Jammes and Paul Claudel. For the young Romanian poet steeped in metaphysics and the poetry of Goethe, Hölderlin, Heine, Shelley, and Byron, the revelations of the year 1916 were profound. History provided a dramatic background to his inner transformation, as Romania entered World War I against Austria-Hungary and Blaga found himself behind enemy lines. As a Transylvanian his sympathies were with the enemies of the empire, out of whose ruins would come Transylvania's reunification with Romania, the mother country. He wrote furiously, trying to break out of "the shell of classical criteria." His distinctive free verse—intended to follow the rhythms of his thought—was born, and Blaga discovered the unique sound that was the signature of his poetry.

In 1917 he was twenty-three years old and had already written most of the poems comprising his first two books. He could have published them at the end of the war, but a strange reluctance held him back. "I recognised that my 'poetry' and 'meditations' did not bring anything, absolutely anything, to the historical realities to which nonetheless I gave myself with all the warmth and purity of youth." An enthusiastic reception by some readers of the manuscripts, including some of Transylvania's most distinguished writers, convinced him to publish *Poems of Light*, however. In 1919 the book appeared to great critical acclaim.

The success of his debut was not without its perils. Blaga's modernist manner, his image-rich poetry, his philosophical pantheism, and, above all, his fresh sound gained him a large body of followers almost immediately. Many of them ended up inventing a pseudo-folk culture that later lent Fascism a certain legitimacy. The group that gathered around the review *Gândirea* (Thought) was responsible for the partial misreading. Blaga's early work contained praise of the unconscious, a youthful cry for pagan health, an exaltation of the old gods of nature, and, like all young poetry, a revolt against the world of the present.

Blaga took his doctorate in philosophy in Vienna with a treatise entitled *Kultur und erkenntnis* [Culture and cognition]. It was the beginning of a distinguished philosophical career that closely paralleled his poetic work. Blaga's philosophy is "poetic" just as his poetry is "philosophical." The two are intimately connected. His theories about culture and metaphor echo in his poems, and the inspired discoveries of his poetry are given rigorous scrutiny in his essays. A third dimension of Blaga's work, his plays, performed on Romanian stages (to varying degrees of bafflement), show another side of this great human writing machine whose purpose, according to its operator, was "the enlargement of the mystery."

"Our duty, when faced by a true mystery," he writes, "is not to explain it, but to deepen it, to transform it into a greater mystery." The credo stands in all Blaga's work. In his poetry, mystery is approached directly through intuition and music, as well as by continuous invention of mythical motifs. "Mythical thinking," a consistently generative principle in his poetry, is also an idea developed in essays such as "The Philosophy of Style" and his three trilogies, *Trilogy of Knowledge, Trilogy of Culture,* and *Trilogy of Values.* Myth and metaphor are the foundations of his world view.

Between 1919 and 1949 Blaga was prominent in the cultural life of Romania. He published a book every year and was, in addition, a prolific journalist. In 1932 he was appointed press attaché to the Romanian embassy in Vienna, after short stints in the Romanian consular service in Warsaw, Prague, and Bern. While abroad he wrote for German newspapers about Romanian literary life. Later he spent a year in Lisbon as first secretary of the embassy before returning to Romania in 1939 to assume a chair at the University of Cluj. In 1949 he was removed from his post. He served as a librarian for the rest of his life. Forbidden to publish his poetry, he translated a great deal from German, including Goethe (*Faust*) and Schelling. Before his death on May 6, 1961, he made a fragile return to the pages of literary reviews, but with poems written in the painfully awkward classical mode he had abandoned in his youth before he encountered European modernism.

Poems of Light and *The Footprints of the Prophet* are the work of a fully conscious voice. The sensuality of his images is reminiscent of expressionism, but the images are only outward expressions of a sensibility that seeks to become one with the cosmos, to leave consciousness behind for a total identification with nature. In an essay on art, Blaga says, "Impressionism reduced man to his retina," then adds, "Van Gogh changed all that by making things partake of his inner life. He ran from impression rendered from the outside, seeking instead the expression charged with the inner soul." The act of animating matter with his soul is Blaga's avowed intention, but there is, simultaneously, a wish to disappear in the pure spirit. Death, sleep, and stasis rule the elliptic world of Blaga's sensual projections. Perspective is abolished in favor of primordial immersion in generative, preverbal energy: "The light what pierces me when I see you, love, / is perhaps the last drop of that light / spun on the first day of creation." ("The Light"). The ontological attraction of this light is a constant in Blaga's poetry. Hell's flames illuminate paradise in "The Light of Paradise". "Between sunrise and sunset / I am only wound and mud" ("Psalm"). "We are guests on the porch / of a new light" ("At the Court of Yearning"). This is light before images, before distinction and individuation, light from which all proceeds and is generated but not yet made manifest. The poet uses his power to prevent manifestation, to stop time. It is a protean and, in a sense, futile operation. Time stops for no one. The poet is one of time's most resolute enemies and, at the same time, a sensitive and grateful observer of its passing in things and seasons. Blaga is a splendid nature poet, and his numerous poems about the seasons, particularly autumn, are ambiguous idylls possessing both infinite regret and immense pleasure.

The many love lyrics scattered through his work are only casually aimed at the beloved, for their primary purpose is to induce an ecstatic joining with the primal stare, a meta-orgasm. Time is of the essence; Blaga's lyrics repair quickly to the garden, where the beginning of the world is always in a state of imminent consummation. The lovers who populate Blaga's woods and villages are constructs for the transport of seeds, quickly unraveling time machines intended to return the world to ecstatic nonbeing. The poet is both demiurge and satyr.

Blaga must have been occasionally stung by criticism of his arrogant disregard for the contemporary world, because he does sometimes introduce the modern world in startling—but stiff—figures, as if doing penance. There is the worker next to his "steel wheels," a figure from the hell of satanic mills, whose "news" the poet spreads willy-nilly. There are "trains" in a particularly chilling poem written on the eve of World War II that prefigures that technological nightmare. Most of the time, however, the "real world" is only the glimmer of distant lights from a horizon, and the poet makes every effort to keep it at a distance. The profound sorrow and wrenching pain of some of his best lyrics come from the knowledge that the contemporary world has already been emptied of spirit, that the poet is pursuing phantoms. The tone of this desolation is a familiar one in European literature, though Blaga's peculiar position at the crossroads of East and West make his accents slightly more profound. His sorrow is for a world *recently* emptied, as if the poet got there only a few moments after the tragic event. The freshness of much of his work comes from the implied nearness of paradise. Paganism has just departed, Christianity had just arrived—but it, too, is being chased away by horrifying machines. The poet, now satyr, now monk, stands in the desert holding the world still. His weapons are silence, sleep, death, stasis, and obliterating sensual excess. There is some kinship here with the atmosphere of Stefan George's poetry, or Miguel de Unamuno's *Tragic Sense of Life*, or even Oswald Spengler's *Decline of the West*, but it is a superficial resemblance only. Their world has already been occupied by reason. In Blaga's world the mythic fertility of the beginnings has left an atmosphere in which the poet has made his home. If Blaga resembles anyone, it would have to be Rilke, to whom he dedicates a touching poem. Expressionism, with its vitalistic and avant-garde offshoots, was the backdrop for these two poets whose sensibilities lay in a great desire to disappear in the mythic collective unconscious. Both felt their condition as one of exile, but where Rilke was in fact an exile, Blaga's exile consisted of an acute yearning for the very place where he was. This place, moreover, retains the imprint of myth in its vacated shell. The poet finds the "footprints of the prophet" everywhere. Every single thing in nature is warm with the bodies of gods. The divine presence flees the poet and expression itself: "Human language, made expressly to trap things existing externally in space, is unable to pinpoint the methodically organized and continuous process woven from the indefinable nuances of consciousness. This process can be caught only with the help of a profound intuition that has freed itself from the mathematical procedures of the intellect, with its categories formed for spatial realities" ("Faces of an Age").

Blaga's poetry ends where stories begin, as he often and carefully reminds his reader. "Tales," "legends," and "fairy tales" occur as signals that we are about to enter the world of the story, the realm of history. "Tales" are bridges from the world of undifferentiated light to the individuated world of mortality. In order to unravel the predictable narrative, to prevent its narrative unfolding, Blaga invents his own stories and myths. Some of his myths are naively medieval, like the frescoes on Byzantine monastery walls: St. George wandering, old, in search of the dragon that all the girls in the villages are in love with. Others are vaguely Greek, staged awkwardly on painted rocks and cardboard caves: Pan grows old with a spider for his only friend. Other stories are texturally folkloric, like the embroidery on peasant blouses. In some of these Blaga walks a very thin line, as one of his most astute critics and a great poet as well, Ion Barbu, pointed out: "I feat that so many motifs in Romanian folklore alter purity rather than reach the complete chemistry of poetry." Barbu may have been right, but in translation, these motifs appear to pin down some specifics in work occasionally threatened by philosophical dissolution. This is one of the very few advantages to the translator that Blaga's poetry concedes.

The difficulties of Blaga's poetry are the difficulties of any poetic world built from the inside, but they are compounded in his case by an almost total reliance on nuance and sound to express "the cosmic, the absolute, the unlimited" ("The Philosophy of Style"). Help comes unexpectedly from Blaga's German education, for it infuses the Romanian with a consciousness that appears quasi-familiar in English.

Romanian poetry, and Romanian culture in general, has always been divided between a French-educated majority in old Romania, and a German-speaking minority in Austro-Hungarian Transylvania. Both these groups have been passionately Romanian, with the Transylvanians often leading campaigns to preserve the Latin purity of the Romanian language. Yet minds schooled in Goethe and Schiller are bound to differ considerably from those steeped in Voltaire and Racine. Consequently, the French-speaking intelligentsia of the capital has always exhibited a quicker and more skeptical turn of mind than the slower and more philosophically deliberate Germanophiles. Translators fare better, it seems, when they translate Francophiles into French and Germanophiles into German or English. But these distinctions are only useful to a point: in some cases they may actually be misleading. Translators have never done will by Tudor Arghezi, Blaga's great contemporary, who is often seen as a nineteenth-century French Symbolist because of his obvious preference for French culture. Arghezi is in reality more like a fourteenth-century monk whose prosody happens to resemble Verlaine's.

The elliptical nature of Blaga's work is the greatest trap for the translator, because it creates a temptation to finish his sentences, giving the poems more fluency than was intended. Blaga is a poet of silences. His pauses, hesitations, dashes, abrupt endings are all part of an unwillingness to give in too much to the realm of the word, which he instinctively mistrusts. His silences are part of the great silence from before the word, and they border all his utterances.

The strong Romanian music of the rhymed poems based on folkloric rhythms is almost impossible to render into English. Where possible I have created a hybrid whose strangeness is meant to flag the appearance of an odd linguistic territory, hoping that by the end of the poem the English-speaking reader will feel at least as welcome as a tourist at a village fiesta.

Many other problems caused previous translators of Blaga to blunder on in blissful ignorance. Being a native speaker of Romanian, however, I had no excuse. In most cases I trance-translated, allowing the words to go from one language into another a little below the level of consciousness, in a sort of musical exchange. Later I took the measure of these dream partners, subjecting them to grammatical tests, eliminated, I hope, much awkwardness. This has also been one of my regrets, for awkwardness is often preferable to clarity. Nabokov believed that only the most literal translations can be in some measure true. I came close to believing this at times. At others, I believed the opposite, that only the most violent remaking can render the original sense. I hope that these swings of translingual violence were to Blaga's benefit. In their final form, these translations would not have been possible without the careful, erudite help of Marcel Cornis-Pop, who painstakingly went through every single word of the poems and pointed out errors, suggested synonyms and different possibilities. I availed myself of his generous help shamelessly.

The present volume includes the majority of Lucian Blaga's poetry written before the Communist era. Missing are only the posthumous poems. The genius of any poetry is fragile because it does not reside in any of its analytically identifiable components. Blaga's postwar poetry appears to have all the "Blagian" elements, but the animating breath is largely missing. The great silence took it back. In leaving out a large body of work by so neatly severing the earlier poet from his later self, I may be committing a sin Blaga did not. But I could not translate what failed to inspire passion in me, after living so intimately and for so long with what I love. For that, I beg to be forgiven.

An original edition of these translations was published by Ohio University Press in 1989. A few months before the momentous end of the year that saw the collapse of the Soviet empire and the end of the dictatorship in Romania. I returned to my native country to report for NPR and ABC news on the bloody finale. Following the return of "normalcy," Blaga's poetry was openly read and received new attention. This book, long out of print, received a new reading by me, as well. I made very few changes to the translation, having to do mainly with my better knowledge of English. Blaga's poetry has grown more urgent and more profound in the decades following its first appearance. This phenomenon is the result of increasing attention to the art itself, but also to Blaga's pioneering engagement with the nonhuman. Romanian poetry, once a terra *incognita*, has become better known in the major languages of the world thanks to the explosion of translation, and fascination with the last century's roots of the avantgarde. Joe Phillips of Black Widow Press has done poetry a great mitzvah by reissuing the work of this major twentieth century poet.

I wish to thank Professors Marcel Cornis-Pop and Matei Calinescu, who closely followed this project, and Peter Givler, of Ohio State University Press who issued the first version. And I thank Joe Phillips for this reissue. I originally dedicated this translation to Mihai Nadin, who claimed some years ago, in Braşov, that I sold him the two-volume set of Blaga's poems when I was still in High School in Romania, but only delivered only one. I hope the translation made up for it. I now add more gratitude to Blaga himself, who often wrote about his posthumous disposition: not only has he not disappeared, but he lives on in my son, who bears his first name.

IN PRAISE OF SLEEP

POEMS OF LIGHT
(1919)

I Will Not Crush the World's Corolla of Wonders

I will not crush the world's corolla of wonders
and I will not kill
with reason
the mysteries I meet along my way
in flowers, eyes, lips, and graves.
The light of others
drowns the deep magic hidden
in the profound darkness.
I increase the world's enigma
with my light
much as the moon with its white beams
does not diminish but increases
the shimmering mystery of night—
I enrich the darkening horizon
with chills of the great secret.
All that is hard to know
becomes a greater riddle
under my very eyes
because I love alike
flowers, lips, eyes, and graves.

The Light

The light that pierces me when I see you
is it not a drop from the light
spun on creation's first day—
that new light thirsty for life?

Nothingness suffered
floating alone in darkness
until the Impenetrable gave a sign:
"Let there be light!"

A raging storm of light
a sea
was born in time then:
thirst for sin, for pleasure, for yearning, for embrace,
thirst for the world, for sun.

Where has that blinding light gone?
Who can tell?

The light that pierces me
when I see you, love,
is perhaps the last drop of that light
spun on the first day of creation.

I Want to Dance!

O, I want to dance as I have never danced!
Let God not feel himself a prisoner in me.
Earth, give me wings:
I want to be the arrow
tearing infinity,
to see only sky around me,
sky above
and sky below—
burning in waves of light
I want to dance
torn by the lightning of unborn desire
so God will breathe freely in me
and will not say:
"I am a prisoner in his dungeon!"

The Earth

We lay in the grass on our backs.
The horizon flowed like the river over the fields,
its wax melting in the bright sun.
Oppressive silence held the earth.
A question dropped into my soul:
Has the earth
nothing to say to me?
This unendurably wide,
murderously silent earth,
nothing?
To hear better I pressed hard
my ear to it—doubtful but humble—
and under the clay I heard
the vigorous pounding of your heart.

The earth was answering me.

The Oak

I hear in the clear distance
the heartbeat of a far-off tower bell—
in its sweet echoes
I feel
that in my veins flows silence
not blood.

Oak on the forest edge,
your soft wings conquer me
when I lie in your shadow
your playful leaves caress and lull me—

Soon perhaps
they will carve my coffin from your trunk,
and I am feeling now
the peace I will taste between its boards—
I listen
silently
as my coffin grows in your trunk,
my coffin with each passing moment,
oak on the forest edge.

The Buds

A fiery evening wind
kisses the sunset sky
brings out the blood in its cheeks.
Sprawled in the grass
my thoughts everywhere
I'm tearing the buds from a spring willow
with my teeth.

I tell myself: "From bitter buds
flower heavy vessels of nectar,"
and warm to my depths I'm chilled
by the bitter flavor of my young desires.

From Your Hair

Once a sage wizard told me
about a veil our gaze cannot traverse,
a spiderweb that everywhere hides being
so we see nothing of what is.

And now as you drown my cheeks and eyes
in your hair,
intoxicated by its rich black waves
I dream
that the wave transforming
the world into mystery
is woven from
your hair—
I shout
and shout for joy
and feel now for the first time
the whole enchantment of the wizard's tale.

At the Seashore

Red vines,
green vines strangle the houses
with savage and lusty embraces—
like squid they squeeze their prey.
The rising sun washes the blood
off the lancepoints which
have hunted and killed
the night.
I stand on the shore
and my soul is gone from home.
It is lost on an endless byway,
it can't find its way back.

Us and the Earth

So many stars falling tonight.
Night's demon holds the earth in his hands
and blows sparks over it
to set it ablaze like tinder.
Tonight when so many stars are falling
your young sorceress body burns
in my arms like a bonfire.
I offer my arms like tongues of flame
to melt the snow of your naked shoulders
greedily suck and hungrily extinguish
your power, blood, splendor, the spring of your being.
At dawn when day will set fire to the night
and the night's ashes be blown away
by the west wind—
at dawn I want us too to be but ashes,
us—and the earth.

Quiet

Such quiet all around I think I hear
the moon's rays tapping at my windows.

A stranger's voice woke in my chest
to sing in me another's yearning.

They say the old fathers
who died before their time
with young blood still running in their veins,
with unquenched desire in their blood,
with a live sun burning in their rage,
come back to live
their unfinished lives in us.

Such quiet all around I think I hear
the moon's rays tapping at my windows.

O soul of mine, who knows in whose chest
you'll be singing to yourself
centuries from now,
playing on strings of quiet,
on harps of darkness,
your smothered longing
and your broken joy?
Who knows?

Beautiful Hands

I foresee
beautiful hands holding my head
with its cargo of dreams
in girlish warmth—
this is the way you will also
hold the full urn of my ashes.

I dream
warm lips will blow to the wind
my ashes held in cupped palms—
your beautiful hands will be flowers
from which the wind scatters pollen.

And I cry
you will be so young still,
beautiful hands.

Tears

When first man,
banished from the nest of eternity,
walked stunned and unbelieving through wood and field,
racked by the admonitions of light, dawn, and clouds
every flower was an arrow reminding him of paradise—
and first man, the wanderer, didn't know how to cry.
One spring,
exhausted by the unperturbed blue above,
he fell into the dust of the road
and his child soul spoke:
"Master, take my sight,
or blur my seeing with a shroud
to hide from me these clouds, and sky, and flowers,
because, you see,
their light hurts me."

And then the All-Merciful in a rare tender mood
gave him—tears.

I Wait for My Sunset

I wash my sight in the sky's
star-filled vault—
I know that I too in my soul
carry many many stars
and galaxies,
miracles of darkness.
But I do not see them
because I have
too much sun in me.
I am waiting for my day to end
I wait for my sunset
I wait for night and pain
I wait for my sky to darken
so that stars may rise in me
my own stars
I have not yet seen.

Have You No Inkling?

Have you no inkling of my madness when you hear
life roaring in me like a stream plunging
into a loud mountain cave?

Have you no to sense of the flame
surrounding you when you tremble
in my arms like a drop of dew
encircled by rays of light?

Have you no warning of my love
when I look you greedily into your abyss
and say, "I've never
seen God so splendid and so grand?"

The Light of Paradise

I laugh into the sun!
My heart's not in my head,
nor is there a brain in my heart.
I'm drunk with the world!
But could so much laughter flower
in my fields
without the warmth of evil?
And could so much enchantment play
on your lips, O Saint,
if the hidden abandon of sin
did not knead your soul?
From whence, I ask myself,
does paradise get its light?
Hell's flames illumine it, I know.

The Shell

I grin and dare myself to look inside,
I catch my heart in my hand
and gather it trembling to my ear,
my treasure.

I'm holding it seems to me a shell
where long unfathomed an unknown sea sounds.

O will I ever reach the shore
of this vast water that today
I feel but do not see?

Three Faces

The child laughs:
"Wisdom and love are my game!"
The young man sings:
"Playing and knowing are my love!"
The old man is silent:
"My love and my play are my wisdom!"

The Dreamer

Tangled in silk
a spider spins in air
between the branches.
A moon ray
woke him from his sleep.
Why does he thrash so?
Did he dream
the moon ray is a thread
he must now climb
until he reaches the sky?
He struggles,
throws himself, and reaches.
I fear he'll fall—the dreamer.

The Eternal

You look for it, astounded.
Bumbling in the dark you sense its trail
inside yourself or in the world.
Yearning finds it in days to come,
resignation uncovers it in bygone nights.

A single unbroken wave hides eternity in darkness.
Nobody sees it, nobody.
And yet everyone can find it
the way I find your lips in the dark, my love,
at midnight when we whisper to each other
great secret words about the meaning of things.

Spring of Night

My beauty,
in the evening when you hold
my head in your lap,
your dark eyes are the spring
from which night flows over valleys,
mountains, and plains
to cover the world
with a sea of darkness.
So black are your eyes, my light.

Thorns

I was a child. I remember
gathering wild roses.
They had so many thorns—
I didn't want to break them—
I believed they were buds
and were going to flower.

Then I met you. O love,
you had so many thorns!
I didn't want to strip them—
I believed they would flower.

All this I review today
and smile—smile
and wander the roads
driven by the wind.
I was a child.

Heart

O heart! Muted witnessings burn deep in her.
I sharpen my astounded mind
to tear its harsh beating,
unlock her understandings.

O heart:
when he plays her mad games to a savage beat
she tells me that from her mud
was fashioned the urn in which
Prometheus set the bright cinder of the gods
while dawn gathered its stars over Olympus
like a miser hoarding his gold.

O heart:
when her fire is smothered in silence
she sings to me that her mud was once the lotus blossom
in which fell the light of a saint's tear—
the first saint and dreamer
to feel the embrace of eternity,
the eerie chill
of understanding that possesses
equally twilight and dawn, sky and sea.

O heart:
when sunsets weigh heavy on her
she whispers to me that she is the mud
where once in Golgotha the blood of Jesus
flowed from the tiny points of thorns.

O heart:
when her pounding threatens to break my chest,
she shouts to me
that over the long and empty centuries
when God will begin
to make another world
and a different people
He will mold the new Adam
from her mud.

The Stalactite

My spirit is silence—
cast in calm I sit,
an ascetic rock—
a stalactite in an immense cave—
the ceiling is sky.
Gently
gently
gently—drips of light,
drops of peace—fall
ceaselessly
to turn to stone in me.

Night

On moon-filled nights, when our wine flasks
sparkle like the eyes of savage beasts,
your honeyed smile stirs the humming anthill
of my desires whose waking allows no rest.
Under the clarity of the night horizon
you look into my eyes and find yourself
savagely mirrored there, brilliant and proud.
Slowly I, oh so very slowly,
I close my eyelids,
secretly hugging your icon in my eyes—
your smile, and light—
on moon-filled nights, when our wine flasks
sparkle like the eyes of savage beasts.

Legend

Bright in the door of heaven
Eve stood
looking at the sky's wounds healing
between branches of sunset.
Dreamily
she bit into the apple
the snake had tempted her to taste
when a seed from the cursed pomme
stuck between her teeth.
She spat it into the wind
and it was lost in the dirt and sprouted.
An apple tree grew there
and others followed it through the ages.
From the rough planks of one of these
master carpenters hewed the cross of Jesus.
O dark seed spat into the wind
by Eve's white teeth!

Spring

Long-fingered the dreamy wind
steals through branches to play
the spiders' harps.
White on your forehead
roses open their damp eyelids,
fresh like the chills
of secret premonitions,
astir with the warm impatience
of your playful blood.

Hungry as always my eyes
call greedily for your
bright eyes—sparkling so
no shadow hides in them.

Longing

Parched, I drink your scent—
I cup your face with my hands
to gather your miracle in my soul.
The closeness of our eyes burns,
and yet you say: "I yearn for you!"
with longing as if
I were a wanderer in another world.

Woman,
what sea do you harbor in you
and for whom?
Sing your longing again and again—
so that I may hear
the minutes burst in bud,
sprouting eternity.

Will You Cry Rivers of Just Smile?

I feel no remorse
for the dirt in my heart—
but I wonder about you—
when a sudden morning
with claws of light
will crush your dream,
your dream of my pure heart
invented by your love.
Will you cry rivers or just smile?
Will you cry rivers or forgive?
Will you cry rivers or give in
to this dawn's claws of light
when I will say without remorse,
"You know that water lilies grow
only in lakes with floors of mud!"

Pax Magna

Why on some bright summer mornings
do I think I am a drop of god on the dirt
and kneel as if to an idol in front of myself?
Why does my self drown like wax
in a great sea of light
in the day's heat?

Why on deep winter nights
when distant suns light up the sky
in the eyes of wolves
does a sharp voice cry in the dark
that nowhere does the devil feel
more at home than in my laughter?

It appears that God and the Devil
knowing how much greater each could be,
shook hands and made their peace in me.
Together they distilled into my soul
faith, love, doubt, and lies.

Light and sin
embraced and became brothers in me
since the beginning of the world,
since angels smashed the flashing
scales of the snake who waits patiently
to sink its poison
into the heel of truth.

Melancholy

A random wind wipes its cold tears
on the window. It's raining.
Obscure sorrows pass—
the pain I feel is not inside
or in my heart
but in the streaking rain.
Wrapped round my body the vast world
with its autumn and evening
hurts like a wound.
The full-uddered clouds glide toward the mountains.
It's raining.

A Fall Will Come

An autumn will arrive one day, a distant fall,
when you, my love, will wrap your arms around my neck
to hug me close and cling from me like a wreath
of dried flowers on the marble columns of a crypt.

A fall will come one day to strip from you
your body of spring, your nights, your longing,
to rob you of your petals and your dawns,
to leave you to the cold and heavy evenings.

A fall will come one day and like a foster mother
will take back all your gifts of flowers
leaving you only those you have not scattered
on the graves of those vanished with your spring.

To the Stars

With the sea of urgings and blind hopes in me,
I kneel before your light, stars—
worshipful flames burn in my eyes like votive candles.
Chills from your remote country kiss
my body with cold lips—I ask you
from my frozen ground: what worlds
and what abysses are you headed for?
The wanderer I am
feels lonelier than the loneliest soul—
seized by a sudden urge I run but don't know where.
A single thought is solace:
O stars, even your spinning has a goal—
perhaps that's why you conquer endlessly.

THE FOOTPRINTS OF THE PROPHET
(1921)

Pan

Covered with withered leaves Pan lies on a rock.
He is blind and old.
His eyelids are flint—
he tries in vain to blink—
his eyes like snails have closed for winter.

Warm dewdrops fall on his lips:
one
two
three.
Nature feeds her god.

Ah, Pan!
I see him stretching his hand—
taking hold of a branch
feeling its buds gently.

A lamb comes through the bushes.
The blind god hears him and smiles—
Pan knows no greater joy
than taking a lamb's head gently
between his hands
to feel for tiny horns under soft wool buttons.

Silence.
Around him the drowsy caves yawn.
Pan catches their yawn and stretching
tells himself, "The dewdrops are round and warm,
the little horns are sprouting,
the buds are full.
    Can it be spring?"

Autumn Chill

The orchard wraps itself in sleep—
from its bushy eyebrows I gather tears:
fireflies.

From the vines of clouds
the moon grows.

My night stretches its autumnal hands to you,
and from the greenish fireflies' light lace
I gather your bright smile in my heart.
Your mouth, a frozen grape.

Only the thin edge of the moon
—if I could kiss it—
would feel as cold as your lips.

You're close to me.

Eyelids flutter in the night.

Autumnal Sunset

From mountain peaks
a red-lipped sunset blows
over the froth of clouds
and stirs the cinders hidden
under their thin veil of ashes.

A ray
running from the west
folding its wings drops trembling
on a leaf:
the burden is too heavy—
the leaf falls.

O soul!
I will hide her deeply in my breast
so that no ray may touch her:
lest she should collapse.

It's fall.

Follow Me, Comrades!

To my friends

Draw near, my fellows! It is fall.
Bittersweet juice ripens in grapes,
and the poison gathers in snakes.

I want to toast the savage miracle leaving me
here with my friends
and with my cry
and fall.

Come closer!—Listen,
if you can:
my suffering's profound only when I laugh.
Let bitterness then
laugh in me today—
and roaring throw its great cup to the clouds.

Come closer, comrades, let us drink!
Ha! What is that eerie flashing in the sky?
Is it the sickle moon?
No, it's a shard from the gold cup
I've broken on the sky
with my steel fist.

I'm drunk and want to pull
down temples, dreams, and altars.

Come near me, friends!
I bequeath to you my beaming skull
to drink from it
the bittersweet juice
when I die tomorrow.
Follow me, friends!

Summer

Over the horizon—far—voiceless lightning bolts
shoot now and then—
spider legs torn from the body of dark.

Sweltering heat.

The earth is a single wave of wheat—
grasshopper song.

The ears of wheat draw grains to them
like suckling babies to their mother's breast.
Time stretches out its lazy minutes
and dozes off among the poppies.
A cricket sings in its ear.

The Cradle

For Mrs. Eugenia Brediceanu

I was so tired
and in pain.
I think I was suffering from an excess of soul.

On the hills dawn opened her eyes
red with sleeplessness.

Lost—I asked myself:
Sun,
how can you still feel the mad joy
of rising?

On that sleepless morning
as I paced with heavy tread
I found a cradle in the hidden corner.
Spiders were weaving their tiny worlds in it,
and woodworms milled its silence.

I looked at it and thought.
It was the cradle
in which a hand grown old over my fate
had rocked
my first sleep and maybe my first dream.
Like a blind man
with fingers of remembering
I touched my past slowly, slowly,
and not knowing why,
I broke down
sobbing over my old cradle.

I was so tired
of spring
of roses
of youth
of laughter.
I searched the old cradle
with delirious hands
for myself—child.

The Thoughts of a Dead Man

I'd like to take time's hand—
feel its slow pulse.
What's new on earth these days?
Do the same stars stream over its face
and do bees still swarm toward the woods
from my old hives?

You, heart, are quiet now.
How much time has passed since you drew tightly
to yourself a new sun every morning
and an old sorrow every twilight?
A day?
Or centuries?

Only a tree above me keeps the light.
Flowers full of milk weigh on my soil.
I'd like to reach out to gather them,
to take them down to me,
but perhaps
the earth has no more flowers.

My thoughts and eternity
are like twins.
What kind of world toils in the day's waves?

Often I hear a muted sound and start.
Could it be my lover's steps,
or has she been dead as well
for countless years?
Could it be her quick and happy steps,
or is it fall on earth,
and heavy, ripe fruit
is falling on my grave
from a tree grown out of me?

Wheatfield

The grains burst from too much gold.
Scattered around red poppy drops—
a girl in the field,
eyelashes as long as barley stalks,
gather bundles of clear sky in her gaze
and sings.

I lie in the shadow of poppies
without desires, needs, remorse.
I am flesh and dirt.
She sings.
I listen.
On her warm lips my soul is born.

Childhood Album

For my little niece Gigi
who likes only rhymed verses

I tended geese with others on the moors.
When I dozed off, a gosling came to take a peek,
and babbling like a child would tease
my earlobe with her friendly beak
among the trembling ancient trees.

When overcome by heat I'd watch through barely open eyes
the bulls slow-steering through the thorns
under the willows—
I thought that they could see like snails
with the tips of their horns
as they hid their heads in the cool grass below.

When I threw myself on my back in the grass
to look up at the vault of the blue sky
I saw myself stretched out against it on my belly,
slow catapult
propped up on elbows.

And I further recall
our scarecrow in the hemp field—
he leaned against the wind for comfort.
He had a purple berry shield—
a sparrow made her fort in his hair.

The children laughed at his rags
but I felt a strange pity for that chap.
For I was young
and thought to myself: "He is my neighbor."
I fancied myself his savior.

At the Abbey

For three days now the moon
has grown like a honeycomb in a hive.

A crone comes to the abbey. Says:
"Abbot, guardian of celestial vaults,
please make a prayer
for the exit of a little soul from the body."

"For whom?"

"For me."

The moon alights on a Bible
and looks up to her face from a page.

An old geezer smelling like frozen wool comes along.
His face is shredded like an ancient papyrus:
"Good Father, I bring a loaf of bread and wine
so that you will kindly pray at the altar."

"For whom?"

"For my flock of sheep."

Later, a girl. Falling stars
or maybe the autumn wind could tell
that once she was beautiful.
"Say a mass, holy abbot!"

"For whom?"

"For my thoughts."

The moon fenced herself in a rainbow.

Give Me a Body, You Mountains

I only have you, my temporary body—
I don't adorn you with blue and yellow flowers—
your weak mud is too small for the terrible
soul I carry.

Give me a body, you mountains,
you seas,
give me a body capable of bearing
my madness in full!
Big earth, be my trunk,
be the chest for this furious heart,
be the shelter for the storms that toss me,
be the vessel of my stubborn self!

My great footsteps will then be heard
in the vast cosmos—
I will be unstoppable and free,
the way I am,
holy earth!

When I make love
I'll stretch all my oceans to the sky,
they will be my rolling, vigorous arms
to take and bend his waist,
to kiss his bright stars.

When I hate
I'll smash under my stone feet
the poor traveling suns
and perhaps I'll smile.

But I only have you, my temporary body.

Poppies

I whistle my joys in bitter elm leaf—
the fear of death enters me
when I survey you, poppies,
from the edge of this sea of rye.

I'd like to gather you—
your petals seem woven
from the red froth
of a burning summer sunset.

I'd like to gather your
boyish courage in my arms—
but so tender you seem
I fear to take you even in my mind.

I'd like to crush you
because you are red, red,
like nothing on earth
but the burning drops of blood
falling on the rocks
and on the sand
from the forehead of Jesus
when he feared death.

Cry in the Desert

With your cries of light,
with the depth of your sea eyes,
with the footprints in your mud
of numberless young girls
seized at this moment by longing,
I call you:
come, World,
come.
Bring to my ears the murmur of those springs
where at midnight the grapes come loose from their clusters
to fill themselves with juice
and after that—with your gifts of death,
come,
World,
come.
Cool my hot forehead
with your burning sand
on which walks slowly
a prophet—in the desert.

Lines Written on Dry Grape Leaves

I. Hafis

In the beginning—we know—the paths of the stars
were drawn awkwardly at random all over the sky.
But then from the arching of your eyebrow
the moon learned its graceful arc over the sea.

II. The Psalmist

When you walk barefoot under the linden,
the pigeons sleeping under the old eaves
wake up believing that your small steps
are seeds thrown to them by a kind hand.

III. Anacreon

The grapes in the red vines are bare breasts
of autumn undressing herself leaf by leaf.
Tear them from their robust vine and squeeze them
into the earth's open mouths—
I want to see your slender hands shaking—
your fingers wet with juice.

IV. The Mystic

Your body and your soul, the high ones,
are twin brothers: they look so much alike
that you can't tell one from the other.
I know only the face of your soul.
Whenever I encounter by mistake your body
I do not know it.
I am confused and take it
for your soul.

The Death of Pan

I. Pan to the Nymph

With a frog for a hat
you jump from the pampas grass—
a wave wants to surround you—
the sand begins to percolate.
You pour your naked body on the grass
from an invisible amphora.

The vein at my temple throbs:
the throat of a lazy lizard
cooked by the sun—
your waving fans me with
the murmur of a spring.

Your movements toss sweet bits of time
into my blood—
your fresh bread I would break.

Sands seethe.

Summer
sun
grass.

II. The God Waits

Mice and calves
play with lambs
in the clearing—
grapevines
hold up
tiny tree frogs.
With a dandelion
between my lips
I wait for you.

All I want
is to comb your hair
with my fingers
with my fingers
comb your hair
and then gather
from the clouds
lightning bolts
like autumn
gathering wisps
of smoke
from cold air.

III. The Shadow

Pan breaks honeycombs
in the shade of the walnut tree.

He's sad.
Churches are multiplying in the woods—
a sparkling cross is bothering him.

Martins circle him,
and the elm's leaves
seem to whistle a church song.

Under the vespers bell Pan is sad.
Moon-colored on his path
passes the shadow of Christ.

IV. Pan Sings

I'm alone, thistles cling to me.
I once ruled over a star-filled sky
and I played my panpipe
to many worlds.
Nothingness tunes its strings.
No stranger seeks out my cave.
Only the freckled lizards
come to visit now,
and sometimes—
the moon.

V. The Spider

Chased off by shining crosses raised in his paths
Pan hides in a cave:
their impatient rays jostle each other
to get to him.
He has no friends,
only a lonely spider.
The little creature spun its silk web
in his ear
and Pan—good-natured—
catches tiny flies for his friend.
Autumns pass in clouds of falling stars.

One day the god is whittling
a flute.
His little friend
is walking on his hand.
In the glow of rotting moss
Pan sees to his astonishment
that his little friend has
a cross on his back.
The old god freezes
in the star-crossed night
and gives a long sigh
felt to the roots
by all living things:
his friend the spider
has converted to Christ!

On the third day Pan shuts the lids
of his once fiery eyes.
Frost covers him
and evening pours out of an abbey bell.
The flute remains unfinished.

IN THE GREAT PASSING
(1924)

Stop the passage. I well know that where there is no death there is no love—and yet, I pray: stop, Lord, the clock with which you measure our undoing.

To My Readers

This is my house. Across from it
the sun and the garden with beehives.
You pass on the road,
look through the slats of the gate,
waiting for me to speak.
Where do I begin? Believe me,
one can speak about anything any time:
about fate, about the good snake,
about the archangels who plow men's gardens,
about the sky we grow toward,
about hate and silence, sadness and crucifixions,
but most of all about the great passing.
But words are the tears of those who wanted
very much to cry and could not.
Bitter are all words,
so let me walk silently among you,
meet you on the road with my eyes closed.

Psalm

Your hidden loneliness, Lord
was always my sorrow. What can I do?
When I was a child I played with you,
I took you apart like a toy.
I grew savage later,
my songs perished—
and without ever being close to you
I lost you forever
in earth, fire, and water.

Between sunrise and sunset
I am only wound and mud.
You locked yourself up in the coffin of the sky.
O if only you were closer to life
than to death
you would speak to me.
From wherever you are, from earth
or story, you would speak to me.

Show yourself in these thorns, Lord,
so I'll know what you want me to do.
Should I catch the poisoned lance thrown
by one who would wound you under the wings?
Perhaps you want nothing.
You are the mute, unmoved identity
(rounded in itself *a* is *a*)—
you ask nothing. Not even my prayer.

Look, the stars are coming into the world
at the same time as my sorrowful questions.
Look, it is a windowless night out there.
What should I do now, Lord?
I strip naked before you. I take off my body
like a coat cast by the roadside.

In the Great Passing

The midday sun holds the day's scales.
They sky gives itself to the waters below.
Passing animals watch fearlessly
their shadows over riverbeds.
Tree canopies arch
over the world's untold story.

Nothing wants to be other than it is.
Only my blood calls through the woods
after its far-off childhood
like an old buck calling its doe from death.

Perhaps she has perished on the rocks.
Perhaps she has sunk into the earth.
I await her news in vain.
Only the caves echo,
subterranean streams call in the depths.

Unanswered blood—
were there enough true silence
you would hear the doe walking in death.

Undecided I stop on my path—
like a killer tying a kerchief around
his victim's mouth
I close the streams with my fist
to make them silent
forever.

Plows

My city friend,
raised in the pitiless city with flowers
in window boxes,
friend who never saw the sun playing
under the flowering pear trees,
let me take your hand,
show you the furrows of time.

On the hills, when you turn,
there are numberless plows, their beaks
planted deep in the earth's healthy flesh,
great dark birds dropped from the sky.
Not to frighten them
you must approach them singing.

Draw closer—slowly.

A Man Bends over the Edge

I bend over the edge:
is it the sea
or my poor thought?

My soul falls deeply
slipping like a ring
from a finger weakened by fever.
Come, end, sprinkle ash on things.
There is no longer a path.
No longer am I haunted by a call.
Come, end.

I raise myself slightly from the earth
on one elbow
to listen.
Water beats against a shore.
Nothing else, nothing,
nothing.

Silence among Old Things

Nearby is my mountain, my beloved mountain.
Among old things
covered with moss since the days of the creation
in the night of the seven black suns
spreading their good darkness,
I should be content.
There is silence in the hoop
that holds together the staves of the sky.
But I remember the time of my nonbeing,
like a faraway childhood,
and I pine for the nameless country
I have forsaken.
I tell myself:
the stars do not clamor loudly.
Yes, I should be content.

The Old Monk Whispers from the Threshold

Young man, walking over the grass of my abbey,
how long before the sun sets?

I want to give up my soul
when the snakes crushed under the shepherds' crooks
give up theirs at dawn.
Did I like them not writhe in the dust?
Did I like them not shed in the sun?
I was everything on earth,
sometimes beast,
sometimes flower,
sometimes a bell—quarreling with the sky.

Today I keep my peace—the emptiness of the grave
sounds in my ears like a mud bell.
I'm waiting here on the threshold for the end.
Will it be long now? Come, young man,
take a handful of dust and sprinkle it on my head
instead of water and wine.
Baptize me with dirt.
The world's shadow crosses my heart.

Daily Rebirth

There is birth everywhere—on the road
and in the awakened light.
My eyes open moist. I am at peace
like fountains in the body of the earth.
Passerby, whoever you are,
raise your right hand over me.
I will not bother any creature today,
no stone, man, or weed.
I'm among nightingales.
Are the old fathers returning?
The prayer begun so many times
can be finished today:
Father, I forgive you for planting me
deep in the furrows of the world.

The day dawns like justice given to the earth.
Flowers too big for words
throw light on my path
from the faraway sea—
halos lost by saints in the fields of time.

Heraclitus by the Lake

The paths come together by the green waters.
Silences crowd here, inhuman and abandoned.
Hush, dog, sniffing the wind with your nose!
Don't chase away the memories that come
to bury themselves, crying in their own ashes.

Leaning on a tree stump I try to guess my fate
from the palm of an autumn leaf.
Time, which way do you go
when you take a shortcut?

My steps echo in shadow
like rotten fruit
falling from an unseen tree.
O the stream's voice is sore with age!

Each movement of the hand
is one more doubt.
Sorrows call in the secret
ground below.

I throw thorns into the lake:
I am undone in the ripples.

A Swan's Call Came from the Sky

A swan's call came from the sky.
Young virgins walking barefoot
hear it among the buds. I also hear it everywhere.

The monks have locked their prayers
in underground cellars. They are dying
under lock and key.

I bleed from my hands, from my soul, my eyes.
I look in vain for something to believe in.
The dirt is rife with the murmur of mystery—
close to the feet,
far from the mind.
I look, I walk, I sing.
To whom shall I bow, who should I honor?

Someone poisoned man's fountains.
Unknowingly I dipped my hands in their waters.
O am I not worthy of living among stones and trees?
Little things,
big things,
savage things— slay my heart

The Soul of the Village

Child, lay your hands on my knees.
I think eternity was born in this village.
Here every thought is slower,
and your heart does not beat in your chest
but deep in the earth somewhere.
Here the thirst for forgiveness is slaked.
If your feet are bleeding
you can rest them in the soft mud.

Look, it is evening.
The soul of the village flutters about us
with its humble smell of freshly cut grass
—a wisp of smoke falling from thatched roofs,
—goats playing between tall graves.

Letter

I wouldn't be writing you now
but the cocks crowed three times tonight
and I too have to cry:
Lord, Lord, whom did I forsake?

I am older than you, mother,
but I have remained the way you know me:
shoulders pulled a bit in,
bent over the questions of the world.

I don't yet know why you brought me into the light.
To walk among things dispensing justice,
to tell them which one is prettier,
which one truer?
My hands hesitate: they are too small.
My voice fades: it is too faint.
Why did you send me into the light, mother?

My body drops at your feet
heavy like a dead bird.

Holding the Great Blind Man's Hand

(variant)

I lead him by the hand through the woods.
We leave riddles through the countryside in our wake.
Now and then we rest on the road.
Clammy snails climb into his beard
from muddy swamp grasses.

I say: Father, the path of the sun is firm.
He is silent because he fears words.
He is silent because each word he speaks turns into a deed.

Under the hard canopy of oaks
bees weave a halo around his head.
And we go on.
Why did he start?
Blind father, keep your peace, there is nothing about,
only a star dropping from the sky its gold tears.
Under the high canopy of leaves we move, farther and farther.
Dark beasts sniff our tracks
and gently lick the earth where we have walked and sat.

Remembrance

I don't know where you are today.
Once eagles flew straight through the gods above us.
It was so long ago—memory's a steep slide.
On the old hills where the sun came out
your glances swept everything high and blue.
A murmur of legend rose from the pines.
The holy pond was an all-understanding eye.
In me you are still spoken of.
Waters flow through my eyelashes still. I should scythe the grass,
the grass where you walked.
I pass through the last gate of sorrow
with the scythe of denial on my shoulder.

Earth's Daughter Dances

I laugh with your dawns,
old sun, new sun.
Fiery birds struggle above us.
Who calls me, who tells me to go?
A-la-la! E-la-la!

There is a church under the green earth.
A thousand years ago
it sank into the ground.
Seven priests say mass even today
for the devil down there.
A-la-la! E-la-la!

Giant mortals, tiny mortals,
I shake the dust from my sandals
onto the crosses stuck on your roofs.
Let the bells toll for the dead.
Nobody can catch me!
A-la-la! E-la-la!

Here I am dancing, too.
Earth's daughter shields
her breasts with a hedge of thorns.
The priests of light,
the priests of the deep
crumble before her vision.

I Understood the Sin that Weighs Down My House

I understood the sin that weighs down my house
like ancestral moss.
O why did I interrupt time and its seasons
differently from the old crone spinning silk in the swamp?
Why did I need a smile unlike that of the stonemason
drawing sparks at the edge of the road?
Why did I covet a different fate
in the seven-day world
from the bellringer's who ushers the dead to the sky?
Give me your hand, passerby,
both you who are leaving and you who are coming.
All the flocks of this earth have
halos over their heads.
I love myself differently now,
as one among many,
I shake myself free of myself
like a dog coming out of a cursed river.
I want my blood to flow down the world's chutes
to turn the wheels
of the celestial mills.

I am vibrating happiness.
All day above me
the winged powers
have pointed their triangles
toward luminous targets.

The Worker

Taut like a bow you waste yourself
beside the big steel wheels.
You crush the breasts of matter in your fists.
Your hands are greased, your dawns smoke-filled.
Worker, in your blue leather apron,
the machines are singing for you,
sweeter than nightingales.

Worker in blue leather apron,
you think beautiful
only things born from human hands.
You know that not one star
came from your hand, but you tell yourself
that poets know nothing,
that no star is truly beautiful.

From fountains drilled into the bones of the planet
you pull your buckets of fire.
I don't know you, you don't know me,
but a light slides
from my face to your face.
Without wanting to I draw close to your news
and shout it to the holy winds.

On the Waters

I freed my pigeons
into the fields of the sky—
torn by winds
they returned.
On the ship's stove
I bury my heart in ashes
to keep the cinders lit.
The firebird does not circle these walls.
The flood goes on.
I'll never make my offering
under the rainbow's high sign.

For an empty honeycomb
I killed my hungry swarms.
The last beast
perished wisely.
His prophetically open eye
is the only news in the dark.
Ararat stays underwater forever,
a sunken sea bottom,
an ever deeper,
more lost—
ocean bottom.

I Am Not a Son of Deed

Numberless are the children of deed
on roads everywhere, under skies and in houses.
Only I stay here useless, fit only
for drowning, if that good.

I am nonetheless waiting, always have,
for a fair-minded passerby, to tell him:
Don't avert your eyes,
don't condemn my laziness.
I grow among you, but shadowed by my hands
the mystical fruit ripens elsewhere.
Don't curse me, don't.

Friend of the deep,
comrade of silence,
I dance over and above deeds.
Sometimes through the reed
of an ancient flute
I sing myself toward death.

My brother looks at me doubtfully,
my sister welcomes me bewildered—
but coiled at my feet
the snake with eyes eternally open
on the wisdom of the beyond,
listens and understands me well.

The Last Word

Tenant of the stars,
I've lost the old celestial signs.
Life, story of blood,
has fled my hands.
Who steers my course on water?
Who guides me through fire?
Who shields me from birds?

Roads have chased me.
Nowhere does the earth
call for me.
I am cursed.

With my few remaining arrows
and my dog
I bury myself in your roots,
God, cursed tree!

Signs

The sign-telling pigeons wash
their soot-covered wings
in the high rains.
I sing—
There are signs, signs of leaving.

White maidens will start
from the earth's cities
for the high mountains.
Following them young men
walk naked toward the sun.
All that has human form
sets out to learn again
the forgotten tales of blood.

I sealed my house with wax—
I won't tarry where games
and crucifixions won't fill
the streets any longer
and no human breeze will
be felt again for ages to come.
The attics will be silent.
Longing will fall from bells.

From the savage outlands
star-eyed deer enter the cities
to graze the meager grass in the ashes.
Elk with huge gentle eyes pass
through the open doors of old churches
and look bewildered about them.

Shed your dead antlers, old elk,
and go from here quickly.
The earth is poisoned here,
these houses once tried
to kill the children who lived in them.
Shake the dust of this earth and depart!
Here—the mad wine of life
spilled into the ashes—
every other road leads into legend,
the great, all-encompassing legend.

IN PRAISE OF SLEEP
(1929)

Biography

Where and when I sprouted into the light I do not know.
From my side of the shadow, I'm tempted to believe
that the world is a song.
A smiling stranger in it, under a spell
I trace my outline with astonishment.
I sometime say words that don't fit me,
and sometimes love things that don't love me back.
My eyes are full of wind and imagined victories.
As for walking, I walk like everyone else:
when guiltily, on hell's roofs,
when guileless, on orchid mountain.

Locked in the circle of an ancestral fire
I trade secrets with the old ones,
the kinfolk washed by waters under the rocks.
On an evening I listen in peace
to the forgotten tales of blood
turning back their course to spill in me.
I bless the bread and the moon.
By day I live scattered in the storm.

With words about to extinguish themselves
in my mouth, I sing—
I praise and sing the great passing,
the world's sleep, the wax angels.
I pass the burden of my star
from one shoulder to another.

Sleep

Whole night. Stars dance in the grass.
Paths draw back into woods and caves,
the hunting horn is silent.
Gray owls sit like urns in the pines.
In the unwitnessed darkness
fall silent the birds, the blood, the country,
the eternally repeated adventures.
In the mild breeze a soul wavers
without today,
without yesterday.
With indistinct waves
rise the hot centuries
from the trees.
In sleep my blood draws me back
into my parents
like a wave.

Falling Smoke

We hear the short hopeless flight
of geese over cold fields.
Somewhere a song draws into itself
ancient chills.
A flute dries up, another never appears.
Praise be, my gaze is filled with birds and wind.
I don't owe life a single thought
but I owe it my entire life.
In interrupted gestures I glimpse
vaults collapsed in deep water.
I come from the leaves of the village
as if from a biblical tent.
Praise be, I am the weary brother
from the sky below
from the smoke fallen from the hearth.

Crumbling Paradise

The winged doorman holds out to you
the charred stump of his broken sword.
He's not fighting anyone
but feels vanquished nonetheless.
Everywhere in the orchards and fields
snow-haired seraphs thirst after truth,
but the waters in the wells
refuse their lowered buckets.
Plowing idly
with wooden plows,
the archangels complain
of the burden of their wings.
The dove of the Holy Ghost
passes among the neighboring suns
putting out the last lights with its beak.
At night the naked angels
huddle shivering in the hay:
woe to me, woe to you,
the water of life is crawling with spiders,
even angels will rot one day under the dirt,
dust will drain the stories
from our sorrowful body.

The Magic Bird

Molded in gold by C. Brâncuşi

High-signed Orion blesses you
in the sudden wind.
A tear shedding above you
its high and holy geometry.

You lived once on a sea bottom
and circled closely the solar fire.
Your cry sounded from floating forests
over the first waters.

Are you a bird? A traveling bell?
Or a creature, an earless jug perhaps?
A golden song spinning
above our fear of dead riddles?

Living in the dark of tales
you play ghostly reed pipes
to those who drink sleep
from black subterranean poppies.

The light in your green eyes is
phosphorous peeled from old bones.
Listening to wordless revelation
you are lost in flight in celestial grass.

You guess profound mysteries
under the hewn domes of your afternoons.
Soar on endlessly
but do not reveal to us what you see.

Equinox

Green signs waver over the fields.
Come, sister, see them shimmer.
Like black monks hailing the sun underground
crickets carry their flutes
into the walls of coffins—and die.
Yesterday we came out of the city
to ask about the new life in front of the gates.
Try not to sigh, good sister, take heart.
In one day the buds and the grass grew
as fast as the nails and hair of the dead.
Where did you, creatures, go, where do you live?
Don't step on their Easter-lily light, sister.

In the Mountains

Midnight find creatures standing asleep
by the abbey wall. The spirit of wet moss
haunts the hollows.
Owl-sized butterflies come from the East
to seek their ashes in the fire.
At the roots of pines, near the cursed hemlocks,
the shepherd lays earth on top of his lambs
killed by the powers of the woods.
Walking over the narrow ridge
shepherd girls brush their naked shoulders
against the moon—
their daring covers them
with the golden pollen they shake from it.

Yellow horses harvest the salt of life from grasses.
Astir under the trees God makes himself smaller
to give the red mushrooms room to grow under his back.
The forest night is a long, heavy dream in the blood of sheep.

Astride four high winds
sleep enters the old beech trees.
Somewhere shielded by deep crags
a dragon with eyes turned to the polar star
dreams of blue milk stolen from sheepfolds.

Old City

Night. The hours turn
without urging.
be still—clock hands
stop—sighing
on the ultimate sign.

Creatures of sleep
crawl under gates—
red dogs and trouble.
On the streets—tall and thin
the rain walks on stilts.

Old weary wind between walls
shakes dirt and iron grates.
Countrymen from bygone times
flash up a moment and vanish.

The black tower stands its ground
counting the years of defeat.
Be still—the stone saint
just extinguished his halo.

Caught in the Game of Returning

On the bank of the Vistula
the farmers look into the eddies.
Oh, under walls, in tree hollows,
what creatures, what whispering!
A thousand years ago
I was the chronicler of changing luck here,
a Romanian refugee seeking the North.

On the bank of the Vistula
I buried my prince in the sand.
Every spring since then
his fingers and temples have burst into fruit.
Here is the tower with drawn bridges.
The iron rooster reminds me with his cry
how often old storms and yellow wind
pass over these roofs.

Transcendental View

Apocalyptic roosters crow—
and crow—keep crowing
from Romanian villages.
Fountains open their eyes
in the night and listen
to the dark news.
The sea washes ashore birds—
angels of water—
On the river bank—incense in his hair—
Jesus bleeds inwardly
from the seven words on his cross.
From woods of sleep
and other dark places
beasts raised by storms
steal in to drink dead water
from old mill pools.
Draped in fields of grain
the earth is a sea of burning waves.
Mythical wings steer frightened
over the river.

In the forest the wind
tears branches and deer horns.
Bells or maybe coffins sing
by the myriad under the grass.

Twilight

Over the same visions, over the same houses,
the vespers bell is heard. I stand at the crossroads
of a lost day. Through the years
what old fires, what new rafts
pass under bridges?

The cloak of shadows pursues me between the walls.
What gate—is unlocked?
What door—springs open?
The ages come to crown me
with a halo of ash.

What friend—late in changed times—
cuts across my path?
What enemy—cuts across my path?
Ah, the phoenix bird does not
fly as it once did over the town.

Bent Head

I urge myself to be
and for a moment I am.
Brother wind died
somewhere outside.

Autumn bleeds
over an old man's walk.
I postpone my meaning
among long shadows.

A flight extended
to who knows what end.
A tree is extinguished
in a sputter of wax.

I bend word and thought
over the deep well.
The sky opens an eye
deep in the ground.

Elegy

The same water, the same leaf
tremble at the chimes of the old clock.
On what shore, in what sleep did you stop?
Under what grass caught, my starry one?

All the roads you walked
flow back into me.
The mirror still holds your face
even after you've gone.

Thoughtlessly, silently, unbidden,
I wipe the wet window with my sleeve.
My neighbor listens through the wall
to the dark patience of even pacing.

Ecstatic Night

Deep under old
green zodiacs—
bolts are drawn
fountains closed.

Cross your
thoughts and hands.
Streaming stars
wash our dust.

Roads

Old city, green spider hovel,
under moss and chutes.
Time sits thinking between
the clock's signs on the tower.
A sparrow struts on its hand.

No echo under the sky vaults.
Your hair plays in the wind.
We met yesterday
in a different city—
it has caught up with me.

Perspective

Night. Under the great spheres
the monads sleep.
Compressed worlds.
Voiceless tears in space,
the monads sleep.

Their movement—sleep sung.

The Saint's Path

"The maidens fell for the dragon" (story motif)

On his iron-plated horse
Saint George looks for signs
on the road—in the wind
he is mirrored
by holy and by evil waters.

Sometimes only a shadow,
other times merely a man,
he blesses bread in the fields,
blesses wine on the hills,
rides in stirrups of trees.

He tightens the iron bit.
The savage sky surges
over seven borders.
Under yellow lawless planets
he stops and does not understand:
his horse lost a shoe three times,
the trees behind him remain
with bare nests under their arms.

An old spirit sings
sweetly under his forehead—
turning into legend
everything he does.

A girl crosses his path
near a well dried by lightning:
Good saint, will you listen?
Don't go any farther, holy man,
because all the maidens in villages and fields
are cursing you with crossed bones,
they hope your lance breaks on his green scales,
they wish the circle of gold on your head
lost in the dragon's well.

Not heeding her, tall like the smoke of an offering
Saint George keeps on going.
At the great water divide
the dragon listens to the deserted borders,
glues his ear to the ground and listens.

On his iron-plated horse
Saint George looks for signs
on the road—in the wind
he is mirrored
by holy and evil waters.

Past Landscapes

In air and water
the castle is one.
The past loses its hounds
at the gate.

Water lilies flit ·
on the shifting roads
carrying in their crowns
the ash of their future.

Escaped from a coat-of-arms
carved on the gate
a hawk interprets
the wheel of fortune.

The astral beekeeper
bends over buckets—
dabs his beard
in the honey wells.

The page boy tarries
in the babble of gardens.
A swallow's flight
signs the landscape.

Century

The underground machines grind on. In the transparent air
unseen transcontinental electric waves
skirt the towers. Housetop antennas
knead space with alien voices and rumors.
Blue signals crisscross the streets.
Lights clamor in theaters, exalting individual liberty.
Crashes are predicted, words end in blood.
They are raffling the loser's shirt somewhere.
The angels come to punish the city
are lost in bars, with singed feathers.
The pale dancer passes laughing through their blood,
balanced on one leg like an upturned bottle.

But on high, six thousand feet up to the east,
the stars tell stories in the pinetree tops,
and at midnight the wild boars
open the mountain springs with their snouts.

John's Immolation in the Desert

Where are you, Elohim?
The world flew from your hands
like Noah's dove.
Even today you wait for it.
Where are you, Elohim?
Troubled and aimless
we look for you in the night's core,
we kiss the star in the dust
under our heels—
we ask of you, Elohim.
We stop the sleepless wind
and track your scent.
We question strange creatures
along the way: Elohim?
We look past the farthest borders,
we saints and thieves,
stones and waters—
we forget the way we came,
Elohim, Elohim!

Palm Reading

At forty—waiting
you will walk just as you do now
between sad stars and grasses—
at forty you will strangle the word
and will be lost in yourself—
still seeking.
The wind will chase you through the years,
you will eat black honey and will be quiet
in your bent frame.
At forty you'll reach the semblance of the shore
where you will forever wait for the other shore
to arrive—perpetual prey
for another horizon's birds.
You will walk barefoot and bareheaded
on seventy-seven old streets.
What seed was not vainly sown?
What light was not vainly sung?

Disclaimers

Trees with supplicant branches
surround an inner sigh.
On all the day's paths
in the slanted smiles of autumn
tall Christs crucify themselves
on crosses of alder.

Skylarks drop heavy from heights,
God's loud tears on the fields.
I question the signs of the far,
round elsewhere.
Sadness is everywhere. Negation.
Denial. The end.

Death leaves her yellow kiss
in my footsteps.
No song urges me to be again.
I take a step and whisper to midnight:
Brother, live, if you will.
I take a step and whisper to noon:
Brother, live, if you will.
No one is being called from my blood
to take up the beginnings of life,
no one, no one is called forth.

White maidens and black maidens
walk the paths of time stepping
heavily like fate.
They are heavenly urgings
to be one more time,
to be a thousand more times,
to be, be!
But I walk by the singing waters,
my face buried in my hands—I resist:
Not me! Amen.

Closing

Each book seems a cured illness to you, brother.
But the one who spoke to you is now dust.
Scattered in water. In the wind.
Or even farther away.

With this page I lock the gates, draw out the keys.
I'm somewhere on high or somewhere below.
Blow out your candle and ask:
Where did the living mystery go?

Do your ears hold a word still?
Turn your soul toward the wall,
Cry in the sunset
The fairy tale of the spoken blood.

ON THE GREAT WATER DIVIDE
(1933)

Native Village

For Ion Pillat

Twenty years later I walk these village paths again—
once I was the little friend of their dust.
I now carry the fever of eternity in me,
the black gravel, the guilty heresy.

No one knows me. Only the wind and maybe
the golden poplar. Poplar rising
like an invisible thread along a spindle.
For two hours the baffled tower will stare
after me until I am lost under the western sky.

How everything's changed! The houses are much smaller
than memory raised them.
The light falls differently on their walls.
The river breaks strangely on its bank.
Gates open only to show surprise.

Why did I return? The branch of my spirit
has not yet distinguished itself,
my happy hour hasn't yet sounded.
The clock tower waits under skies not yet built.

Sickness

A sickness enters the world,
nameless, faceless.

Is it creature? Or wind?
No voice can tame it.

Man is sick, stone is sick.
Tree is extinguished, fire put out.

Wretched sod, black silver,
sick, diminished gold.

Obliquely fall the century's tears.
I invoke forgetting and healing.

Yesterday's Light

I search, for what I don't know. I look
for a past sky, for a young sunset.
How humbly bends the arrogant forehead
of yesterday's ecstasy!

I search, for what I don't know. I look
for rainbows that once were lit fountains
—today their water is sealed and still.

I search, for what I don't know. I look
for a great hour left creatureless inside me
like the stamp of a dead mouth on a carafe.

I search, for what I don't know. Under spent stars,
under vanished stars, I look
for the extinguished lights I still praise.

Autumnal Signal

Yesterday from the depths a voice rose,
bitter, bitter, bitter.
Many angels dying have added
their clay to this country's clay.

Yesterday a heavenly signal was given
in the circle of deceit.
And then the wind and swallows
were seen leaving for Saturn.

September

Forgotten poisons breathe
in the green hour of the forest.
Late-blooming crocus
grows by eerie eyes.

The stream tries again
to learn the old song.
In the moist moss stir gently
the forgotten traces of my youth.

Great herds come chiming
through the evening of round oaks
making the forest echo
with the sound of lost churches.

The tall voiceless unicorn
tarries in the sunset to listen.
Under their deep canopies the woods
kill me with rushing horns.

Sick Music-Makers

Tearlessly we carry a tune,
an illness in the string—
we walk without surcease
toward the rising moon.

Our soul is a sword of fire
spent in the scabbard.
Ah, over and over
the words dry in their husks.

The eternal wind blows
in the mists of the firs.
We reached this world
on the bridge of a ballad.

We cross the sunsets
clenching white flowers.
We lock our ends
within our armor.

Tearlessly we carry a tune,
an illness in the strings—
we walk without surcease
toward the rising moon.

We carry wounds—streams—
hidden in our fiddles.
Endlessness grows
from strings' riddles.

Enchanted Mountain

I enter the mountain: a stone gate quietly shuts.
Dream and bridge fly me up.
What violet lakes! What vital time!
The gold fox barks from the ferns.

Holy beasts lick my hands: strange,
under a spell, they stalk with eyes turned within.
Buzzing through the sleep of crystals
the bees of death fly. And the years. The years.

Beach

The cedars and sycamores feed
their generations in the sea.
Wide purple furrows stretch
under watery plows.

Air and harbor, fishermen and custom clerks
—all doze in the roomy heat.
The white wind squints with one eye
at its own shadow on the opposite shore.

Lost in the rarefied hour
I look through the thorns of the door—
naked people lie in the sand
quietly, as if in their own ashes.

Playing with a stone now and then
a wave shows the scales on her belly.
Between the high sky and earthly poisons
sickness seeks me out like a song.

Mediterranean Evening

Barely glimpsed lighthouses
signal out at sea.
Wasps enclose themselves
in crystals of wood.

Gripped by an unknown pain
the bitter thorn
digs deep into the ground
like a writhing hand.

The warm south flows softly
through broken urns,
through the blood,
through a faraway flute.

Nightingales come
singing from Hades
and alight on the table
between bread and wine.

Border

The Milky Way, barely glimpsed, disappears,
written in the scorching and calm night
like a runic lifeline
carved on an immense and patient hand.

The Acheron flows under celestial vaults
peaceful like everlasting icon oil.
Who will now begin the song of the crossing?
To whom will the black water now give pitch?

Scared seagulls rise from the darkness
when the boat of shadows slides by.
Souls aflight knock against my forehead
rasping like beetles in late summer.

Everything is done. Seven times twisted
Acheron breathes deeply in his sleep.
Who will now begin the song of the crossing?
To whom will the black water now give pitch?

Spell and Curse

On the ridge of night the dry mill
grinds empty light.
Its paddles dance up and down.

The loom behind the door
weaves by itself—see any spindle?
Make the sign of the cross to the west.

From wells on evil alleys
buckets are lowered and lifted
toward the plundered sky.

Tree nests go up in flames
lit by an unseen hand.
Hear the eggs explode.

The evil spirit keeps sneaking back
to the deserted village to graze
in the forlorn commons on the grass of dead men.

In the old village by the moon
doors open, doors close.
My shadow falls on the wall.

The Train of the Dead

As the night is long and wide
no dog barks.
Only glowworms in the thorns
join light with neighbor stars.

Glowworms with green lanterns
give right-of-way to a train
that will pass through the cities
into the great, cold horizon.
The coming train
that no one will hear.

Divine Touch

What vision! Ah, what light!
A white star fell into the garden,

Unexpected, unsought. Luck,
arrow, flower, fire.

In the high grass, in the wide silk,
it fell from the house of time.

A star came back to our world.
My hands bear its scar.

Questions for a Star

Star, barely glimmering under the Big Dipper,
stunned between seven big lights, whose are you?
Are you the Green Emperor's star—his restless ghost?
What holy day do you protect? What full hour?
Do you guard a grave or a healing water?
Do you protect a nation, a city, or only a flower?
Over what soul, what blessed crop,
do you hold your dim light in the big vault?
If you are mine, guarding my time and my home,
see that no one makes after you with a stone

Runes

From the oldest time each creature
bears a signature in runic script.
The holy birds have it under their wings
in their lifelong flight.
Serving light, earless urn, the moon,
keeps it hidden on the face
spellbound never to turn.

Stone idols, beasts, elder trees,
are signed with a lost key.
You, fire-girl, vision,
carry your double-sealed print
under your arms
raised toward the sea.

Runes, everywhere runes,
who inscribes you, who sets you in place?
All creatures, seen and unseen,
sport their signature—who can undo it?
High mountain lilies—sublunar—
carry it on their tallest petal.
Our mothers carry it on their foreheads.

Birth

New creature, look,
the first light licked your face.
You reached us without taking a step
as fate hurries us along.

Creature from nowhere descended
in the spaciousness of mother earth,
golden, young, fresh vessel
broken from ribs of mud!

Worried, bewildered, triumphant,
we will surround you.
Your light will grow in us
great like the faith
with which you have chosen us!

The waking stars on high
light their coals against evil.
Under the eaves of the world
you'll slowly bloom, like a tear.

Archangel Returning Home

I return now
like a bee to its hive,
with grace under wings,
with sunset in my blood.

On the world's scales
a day weighs down
rich in events,
without guilt.

Each time I tread
the beaten earth,
mud lips
kiss my feet.

I return now
to the light of my hearth.
My deep ricefields
bow to the wind.

On the Great Water Divide

Your summer is here, my summer is here. Both
balanced in the season about to end, on the great divide.
You caress the earth's hair in playful thought.
We bend over the rocks in the unfinished blue.

Look down on the world! Look long and be still.
Our voices could easily falter.
How quickly the water goes gray
from the heights to the valleys—like the clock.
Is it far back? It's the same ahead,
only it will seem much less.
We hide—burning low—behind a summer illusion.
We close our hearts around unspoken words.
The path descends now like smoke
from a refused offering—we take it
down to the valley, betrayed a thousand times over
for the siren song of an unvanquished sky.

In the Woods Unheard

In the woods unheard
cries a sick bird.

Stiff in cold weather,
nothing makes her better,

unless she drinks some dew
with ash, from a burnt star.

She keeps gazing, not much good,
at that star above the wood.

De Profundis

Mother—nothingness—the great! Fear of it
shakes the grounds under me night after night.
Mother, you were once my grave.
Why do I fear
leaving the light again?

Carol

For Dorla

The fatherless child
sleeps in the pen.
His mother cries
and tells the cow
that he has no linen
no water no blanket
no candle no nanny.
Joseph hung his halo
on a nail by the door
and took off somewhere
to the bark of strangers' dogs.
The hour is long, the night is black.
Mother watches over baby.
A tall angel comes down
to keep them company.
To comfort them
he lights his finger.
God's angel burns
like a wax candle.

The Bear with the Lily

He's resting under the abbey's plums, sniffing
the ancient wind. Yesterday a girl gave him a lily.
He will travel through thousands of villages.
They will offer him holy bread on wine-blessed roads.
The sick will drag their bones to meet him on his path.
He will tread away evil. He will dance for health,
mumbling forgotten words over them.
By evening sickness will leave their homes, thoughts, and flesh.
He has an ambling step when he walks, like a king.
Under his west-gazing forehead is amber with a golden core.
As he moves his paws right and left and now left and right
he seems to be dividing the forests he owns in the high country.

The Outlaw

He lives in the wood, in the green country.
He ponders a moment with his hand in his beard.
His mind wanders off to thoughts of gold, blood,
and he weaves himself rings from a special weed.

From now on he must cut across every path.
He will be lost in the mountain, he will be lost.
He'll forget about his mother, or his death.

He will go ever more deeply to the place
where autumn locks its serpents in stone.
He will unfetter the spirit of the wood
and the singing of the gushing springs.

No one will see him for many years.
The hawk will overcome him with a cry.
The owl will mark him with quick screeches.

Country

Oil wells and blue vineyards
grow on hills to the sun.
Our rivers take golden grain
to feed other nations afar.

This country has pushed
its borders to the sky.
Eagles revolve—minute hands
of the eternal clock—
over shepherd and field.

Fluttering like flags
in their saffron dresses
girls burn in midsummer
in the laughing year's wind.

AT THE COURT OF YEARNING
(1938)

At the Court of Yearning

Our vigils: flour sifters.
Time passes through—
white dust in our hair.
Rainbows still catch fire:
we wait. We await
the solitary hour
to share in the green
kingdom, the sunlit heaven.

We are still:
wooden spoons forgotten
in the gruel of long days.

We are the guests on the porch
of a new light
at the court of yearning,
neighbors of the sky.

We wait to catch a glimpse
through gold columns
of the age of fire—
our daughters come out
to crown the doorways with laurel.

Now and then a tear springs up
to bury itself painlessly in the cheek—
who knows what pallid star it feeds?

Years, Wandering, Sleep

The years will grow longer,
shuffling slowly
from city to city.
I stop to gaze at the meager dirt.
These years of boundless exhaustion,
wanderings, bitter lights,
will, I believe, drag on forever,
like a wind that clothes
and hurls me forward.

I cannot build from this wandering
the foundation once promised,
the firm shore—
no new rocks are heaved forth
from the earth in my wake.

I've been to all sorts of places
all the way to the Northern Circle,
where the axis of the heavens
groans in the terrible cold.
I slid through the pines
with meager shadows
under the sign of Capricorn.
Nations, everywhere different,
lit their various fires
under suns pushing unfamiliar skiffs.
Fate used all its flags
to surround me with an uncertain horizon
whose toy I've become.
I am imprisoned under foreign sky
by the clay of dark luck—
it will not let me go.

I see the years grow, my stride lengthen
over valleys, ridges, winters, summers,
over bells and silences.

The deserts call, the hills tempt me.
Only my hearth is forbidden—
ah, how I would sing its earth-bred spark,
its custom and ash, its high smoke!

I stand turned toward my country—
return is a dream
I cannot wake from—
I am caught in its writing.
Only at night, each night, late,
sleep comes from the far-off plains,
bringing me a cupful of darkness
like a fistful of dirt from my mother's country,
from the heavenly cemeteries.

Anno Domini

Night came into town without paying the toll.
It snows again under the graying hours.
Medieval goblins of the woods
sulk under the eyebrows of cathedrals.

The tolling of the hours startles the bat
from the long sleep where he has settled.
The ash of angels burning in the skies
falls softly on our roofs and shoulders.

Near the City

The town fool looks at the clock tower.
How busy is time, how smoothly
its poison dwells among us?

Boing-boing! It would be good
if the city forgot its master
the clock tower for one day!

Whose victories do not spoil?
Whose heart does not stand still?
Ah, Acheron's wave is pointing
all our rowboats to the sunset.

With the Old Ones

If you put your ear to the stones
you can hear golden scarabs kissing
the ancestral mud
where our branches fell deeply
into bitter cold regions.

If you put your ear to the stones
you can hear worms storming the paths of time
to enter yet again in holy communion
with our flesh Sunday after Sunday.

Raven

White field. A raven dives
from the milky smoke.
Do you see him, Ana, my little girl?
In autumn around here the golden story wound down,
the squirrel jumped, the chestnut fell.

The raven measures his step, writes in the snow
some new gospel, or maybe some celestial news
for someone who might pass through the country
and has not forgotten how to read.

We humans have.

Mountain Lake

In the mountain funnel the hidden eye
of the calm mountain lake awoke—
it mirrors high flight and the clean
hour it has once been promised.

It looks long to the north and the bygone days
and then sweetly at the leaden sky—
it dreams afternoons of the gold fruit seasons
baking serenely in the terrible cold.

Awakening

The tree starts. March echoes.
The bees gather and mix in their combs
awakening, honey, and wax.

Unsure between two borders,
its veins reaching under seven fields,
my tree, my chosen one, sleeps,
dragon of the horizon.

My tree.
The wind shakes it, March echoes.
The powers join together
to relieve it of the weight of its being,
to raise it from sleep, from its divine state.

From the height of the mountain
who sifts to cover it with so much light?

Like tears—the buds overwhelm it.
Sun, sun, why did you wake him?

Good Tidings for the Blooming Apple

Joy to you, apple blossom, joy!
Look, all around you, finely spun gold
like a wisp of cloud.
Fine threads burst from an invisible spindle
from everywhere and nowhere.
No creature is doubtful—the pollen
fallen like burning embers into their cups
is sweet torment to all flowers.

Be glad in the blossom
and understand—
We don't have to know now
who brings and spreads fire.
I'm an angel, you see, and you are a flower.
If you ask me, I cannot keep still
and rein my voice in.
Who brings this, the tremor, the heat?
Who else, but the wind?
It's the wind, the invisible prince,
the one without hands, without body,
ruling over the days of the week.
Joy, apple blossom—
fear not your fruit.

Uninvited Guests

The Dacian kings left again
for the north—returned
with sheep and cattle.
The others came from the east
with camels and slaves
and stayed over later
as evening fell.
The maiden isn't very surprised
that she's lost her slippers
in all the frantic to-do.
Mary wants peace
after all the guests,
she wants quiet, and the quiet
joy to be herself, alone.
Perhaps she should blow out
the star lit over her gate.
She alone is at fault
that so many guests are drawn hither
from the four winds.
Of this very same serene opinion
is also the old mule
while he chews to bits the slippers
he found in the hay by the door.
Mary hasn't even found the time
to see her baby yet,
with so many emissaries.
She bends over the manger
and over the light.
From too much love
milk bursts from her breasts
and soaks her blouse.

Lark

Someone is singing with the dawn
on this cloudy day. Who is it?
Someone is singing on the horizon.
Is it bird? Is it spirit?
It can only be he,
the little earthly one,
with his much praised
festive body,
his sky-clear voice,
the hosannah blood.
It can only be he:
the Christ of birds!
He who rises every day,
conquers without steel,
from the wheatfield to the sky,
to undo the sins
of all our villages.

The Village of Miracles

We bumbled our way through stubble fields
and dusty paths to the place where few
arrive without maps. We often
followed silence and the blue way
of the moon, missing the obvious road.

At the wells of the gift of grace
illnesses are smoldering, birds shriek.
The village is full of the god's scent
like a nest filled with animal warmth.

Overturning laws and customs
the miracle shoots forth like a poppy in rye.
Danubian roosters perched on old fences
broadcast the news of an endless Sunday.

Pond

The fish gather
in front of the spirit
eyes turned
to the moon.

Gold spindles
little water gods
they learn from the moon
how to be silent.

Plenty

Hey, black cherry tree,
they're plotting against thee.
Mouths arriving from the night
crave your mysteries full ripe.
Man, birds, and ghosts are needy.
They aren't waiting till you're ready.
You're too full of fruit and charm.
Be on guard now against harm!

Let them come and pick me bare!
I still have the summer air.
Nobody can hope to steal
the stars above the hill.

The Song of the Pine

Under the Big Bear, smothered by moss,
untouched by man, unreached by hawks,
old, old, in my kingdom,
the bearded pine stands guard.

Ferns and owls and wasps inhabit it.
Holy spiders move their fogs through him.
Every new century, from on high,
a white bolt of lightning strikes him.

Between celestial seasons and country
stands this pine—kissed by lightning.
His branches burn, but look, from the ash
new evergreen branches are sprouting!

A wild pig from a fairy tale sharpens
his plaster tusks against the bark.
Unmindful of sunset in my kingdom
the young pine is always on guard.

1917

The firing ceased. It was a day of rest. From the trenches
we looked at the tangled land, the orchard in flower,
the rags on the barbed wire. We felt Easter in the quiet.
Once more, ten comrades, we lay in a hole, a rudderless boat.

Rare creatures, a cloud of butterflies, rush in from the west,
fly over our heads in high swarms
playing, clean, high, sparkling, going over us in swarms,
playing their clean, sparkling colors saved
from another continent, now buried and gone.

Tomorrow the battle starts again. Turn to wood, heart,
when each silence is a question: on which mountain
will the first of us fall?—Each of us wished
to read a sign on his comrade's brow.

Only I say to them: Keep your peace! Tomorrow at dawn
not men but flowers will be the first to fall.
The Easter lilies with the purple blouses,
and the dandelions with gold helmets like ours!

Destiny

The cranes are leaving for the fiery climates,
their cries barely heard above the country.
They row on high as if pulled on the stake
of a moon ray.

Tomorrow they'll be at the water crossings.
They'll float asleep in the shadows for days.
Brief lightning discloses them in the night
above the seas welling from legends.

Marine Sunset

The evening frolic of dolphins
vanishes in the play of lights.

The wave covers up names written in sand
and erases the path of my hand.

The sun, God's fiery tear,
sinks in the ocean of sleep.

The day is cut short, and the news.
The shadow makes the stories grow huge.

The star touches you with her lashes.
Quietly you read her signs.

Ah, for whom does the time expand?
For whom are meant all the masts?

O, adventure, great sea-lanes, skies!
My heart, shut tight your eyes!

Estoril

Houses grow in the pine forest
beaming white and saffron orange on hills.
Calmer now the ocean caresses
the sunny places.
The horizon welcomes the ghostly rowboats.

With arched brows only the old palm trees
still sway delayed in yesterday's storm.

Dressed in smiles and gold
Cora embroiders under the shadow
of the oleanders' long leaves.
How easily you could catch time
as it leaves your house on a silk thread.

This is peace. Peace for the heavenly
kingdom to do its growing in us.

Longing

For Bazil Munteanu

For hours, for days, I stand watch
on a yellow Portuguese shore.

My armor is straightened and ready.
My arms are crossed on my chest.

For seven years singing my *doinas*
I contemplate the lambs in Lusitania's sky.

Perhaps the restless windmill
won't find me on this hill.

Perhaps I won't vanish unseen
into the blue and always serene.

Atlantic Breeze

At dawn with quickening silver shoes
the mules suddenly batter the streets.
The phantoms hastily dismantle themselves.

On the quays the sibilant voices awaken.
The light waits for its cue to drown
the boats, the churches, and the hills.

From the port with the din of the tides
the fishermen arrive with their baskets
on their heads: squid, rainbows, conch.

The Atlantic breeze roughs up the mills,
the midcentury, the milk of the sea,
the women's hair, ashes, and flowers.

In the rose pearl morning only
one solitary heart chooses to cross
all by itself the sun's season.

The Grasshopper Peddler

The avenue echoes at night: GR'OPPEH! From the fields
the peddler enters the city on a mule, with grasshoppers
in his hair, on his arms, crawling on the sides
of his full baskets. He's going to sell them at the market.
He looks about him awkwardly and squints.

To sell he needs a stamp of field in the city
and a new song for chimneys and houses.
The swarm on his shoulders is living black silver.
Gr'oppeh! Gr'oppeh! Precious sound, collected afar!

It is thus that they make their entry into the city,
into the loud grid of its veins, unabashedly
singing—the country's grasshoppers!
My lonely little girl, luminous Ana, hears them at night
and smiles in her sleep at the moon and the sea.

The Unicorn and the Ocean

Shyly the unicorn comes close to the shore
looking long at the sea, at the farthest wave.

He'd like to draw back but is licked by a wave,
and the silver-spurred mystery pierces him.

The unicorn on the shore suspended in time
confronts the ocean inside a fairy tale.

Is this water, or a being with powerful breath,
in whom he feels himself sinking to his knees?

He bolts in fright all the way back to the wood
when the mystery shatters from bottom to crest.

The Sun Coast

To Vasile Băncilă

Leaf-green, dear leaf-green hills, love,
you gather tightly the lights above.
The waters sing, the great waters.

Horses' hooves pass on the road,
desires pass quickly through thought.
The bird on the crag breaks her fetters.

Handsome, lean like spindles,
graveyards turn out glances
to hearts lost to old winters.

Still are the windmills,
thought, the graves on steep hills.
Leaf, mast, hour burn deeper.

Return

Here I am in the village again,
comrade of its shadows.

I find myself again on the old
path of beginning, the ancient.

How changed all is—man, hearth!
Only the village is unchanged,

after so many Aprils and autumns,
unchanged like you, Lord.

The hazelnut shakes her gold.
The flute speaks. Smoke falls.

Our fathers' grasshoppers
sweetly sing, sweetly die.

With its scent of dear poison
the alder stirs memories.

The narrow leaf reproaches me long.
The wind tastes my tear quickly.

THE UNSUSPECTED STAIR
(NEW VERSE, 1943)

.

Monologue

Welcome the new year! Turn over the furrow
and stretch it dreaming all the way to sunrise.
The fruit will fall fully ripened into your hand
the way every spell ends with a round Amen!

All the busy springs and fire,
are borne aloft in the hand of the All-High.
You need add only faith to your step,
and reverence, care, and buoyancy.

Welcome the new year! Increase your being
past that crude border that wants to abolish you.
See, the dust of the passage clings to you
just as it does to the wake of the moon.

Make your song grow to fit your wide stride,
give the hour the wisdom you have in abundance.
The dream of golden luck is handed to you under the eaves
by the house snake and field gods.

May 9, 1895

My village, whose name holds
the sound of tears,
answering the deep calls of mothers,
I have chosen you one fateful night,
as threshold of my world
and path of my desire.

Whoever guided me to you
from the depth of the age,
whoever called me to you,
let him be blessed,
my village of unhealed tears.

Self-Portrait

Lucian Blaga is mute like a swan.
In his country
the snow of being fills the place of the word.
Since the beginning
his soul has been searching,
mutely searching
to the last frontiers of the world.

He is searching for the water the rainbow drinks from.
He is searching for the water
from which the rainbow drinks
its nonbeing and its beauty.

Note: The poet's native village is Lancrăm. The Romanian word for "tear" is lacrima.

My Little Girl Looks at Her Country

Ana my golden shadow
Laurel dowser laurel

I gather you from sunsets
High road low road

Cull your first meanings
Under lashed summer hours

And you look and see and see
The robust young year to be

To his trees to his beginnings
You send kisses and give names

Stunned by voices flowing water
Finger buds touch garden shovel

In your new world all is shiny
New leaf man dew and tale

White bead rising in hot circle
Snakes in awed magnetic sunsets

How you wonder can they be?
How can all these wonders be?

Only good or bad the moon
Seems to you the same old moon

Changing Season

I told myself often:
it is but memory—of a past hour.
No more dreams for you, poet.
No light no star no power stays.

Forget Arcadia. Forget the hour
that will not sound, the not-yet rounded
hour, the unfulfilled unborn hour.
In your fog wheat does not ripen,
at your fountain pitchers do not fill.
Barely does word filter from
the world the sun rules.
Others are always holding
the legend.
Miracles are elsewhere,
stars are increasing their distance.
You are surrounded by No!
Sink into the kingdom of darkness,
keep to your own thresholds.
Under the low uneventful horizon
your years of sorrow unfold slowly.

So I tell myself often
crushing a flower underfoot
or treading the startled shadow of some dirt god
who crosses my path but cannot stay.

Even yesterday, only yesterday
I defended myself in terror
of the new rising sky.

And today unexpectedly the sun rose.
What measureless song!
My world expands in the light
of cured blindness.
Powers move the breaking horizon.
Gates open: Welcome untraversed time,
Welcome!

The Pleiades

I count the stars in the Pleiades
At night I count them and count them.
The sky signs my right shoulder.
One moment I am, the next I am not.
The wind lights them, blows them away
Someone set them in a cross.
The wind burns them extinguishes them
sets them loose in my blood in my mind.

Fire play, heart play.
I am tired of counting over again
the star points the minimal stars.
Great fires, serene great fires.
As many hearts as I can see
Beat in space for me.
Great hearts great serene hearts
Burn in the valleys and on the hills.

Spell

Mistress from far Barsa plain,
I'm all light and loving pain.

I'd send news for you to see
what poison mixes with my ecstasy

in the bowl in my pantry,
Mistress from far Barsa country.

I'd send you these black flowers
from dreams born at early hours

but I fear that you'd mislay
my flowers in the sun in anybody's way.

Better to keep them hid and shady
so their high and somber beauty

may grow under a magic star.
I'm all light, a living scar.

Noble Maidens

One day the princess of this legend
asked me,
"Do you know who Uta was?"
A sun older than our diurnal sun was setting,
increasing the towers of the Black Church.

I know her, yes, I know her,
the noble maiden praised in early Middle Ages.
She is the comrade of my shadows
who lived once hereabouts.
She lived tall, white, and quiet
by her lord's shield.
Uta lived under the pale embroidery
defending her being.
Her smile poisoned all the valleys of the Rhine.
She only left her city in the fall.
Her beauty caused the country great suffering.
Burgundy suffered where now her stone figure rests.
It was written that she would be the aim of this dream.

I took the hand of the princess and told her:
This finger could have worn
the terrible ring, the fierce medieval gold circle.
Your flames are alike.
You carry from place to place
blood, laughter, luck, fire, misfortune
just as she did.
When you pass through the tall grasses
you start fires in the dew
just as she once did.
But I shouldn't perhaps
follow every path of the thought-song
balance all its lights
break out all its meanings.

Princess, our words are tombs.
Tombs in which time locks its sorrows
when beauties try to arrest its passing,
wounding it with their bitter charm.
It would be wise to refrain from words
under these arches, these blessed arches,
wise not to play by the graves.

The Poet

In memory of Rainer Maria Rilke

My friend, let's not call him
by that useless name mortals used.
The poet no longer has a face or name
now when he speaks to all of us.
His life troubled us
with its hermetic song,
its meaning hidden in strange weave.
Years ago the poet strangled his words.
He bore misfortune in manly quiet.
On the peak of solitude where he lived
he put out the flames of many sorrows.
When at the urging of an invisible sign
the blue depth of the sky collapsed
and the minute hands of time
sliced through his being
the poet cried to forget his seed.
In those years of terrifying gloom
when numberless human beings
streamed from their flesh and homes
so much life was extinguished
that spirit itself almost took earth to itself.
The poet, his name erased and lost,
retired under the mountain,
made friends with the tall stone crags.
Great and alone
he stood still but remained
in the play of destiny,
flanked by black and white seasons.
He was not killed by the bitter pain in the valley
nor by the thought that God might have broken
his will to embody.
Neither darkness nor lightning touched him.
He was not burned to ashes by the lightning bolt
who was for a moment his guest.
His walk was tied

to the word he kept to himself.
My friend, let us remember
that the poet died only much later.
Much later—killed by a thorn
dipped in sky blue,
a fiery bee sting.
The poet died killed by a rose,
by a thorn dipped in simple blue, in light.
Since then the puzzled nightingales
have fallen silent in the thickets.
The hour's nightingales in our meager gardens
were silenced in the light that came without signs.
They know nothing on earth
that will make them
sing again.

Magic Sunrise

This is the way it was, the way it will be always.
I wait with my flower of flames in my hand.
Disturbing my greatly exaggerated weeks
the moon powerfully rises.

An earthquake shakes the midnight spheres.
In space—rivers, shadows, towers, hooves.
The hieratic star liturgically undresses the country.
Up there in the light how fragile the mountain!
The gods' cities crumble in the eyes of children
like old silk.
How holy matter is,
all sound to the ear!

Urging to a Tale

From the scorching weather
of the fairy tale
I invoke you, unicorn,
with a secret sign.
I hear your hooves
in the tired green,
deep-wood fresh,
crisp temptation.

Don't run cautious circles,
don't ponder or wait!
Leave now for the city,
propitious messenger,
when the clock tower strikes.

When you enter
take heed of the lonely house
just past the toll bridge
see the house
where my fair one lives.
Knock on her gate
with the sound of fate.

Touch her locked door
three times with your horn.
Kneeling
make the sound of healing.

Touch the stone
of her threshold.
And if she permits
see her in her cradle of sleep.
Touch her forehead
her cheek her eyebrow
her tear-wet kerchief
her pillow of sighs.

Let her gaze
and her hand
pass through
your halo.

Let me know with a neigh
when everything's done.
Leave then this city
for the peace of your forest.

The Colt

The colt jumps in play, jumps in the well-filled corral.
He is black—like a cygnet. Like the spring field.
Soon he will be white like the cloud trailing him.
He was born under the shield of Saint Wednesday.

He stirs up the dust in the yard when he catches
the dark scents of the earth in his nostrils—
he remembers the almond-dark taste
of his mother's bitter milk.

He stretches to smell who knows what high meadow
but then urges himself back to the coals in the hearth.
The silver from which I will make him horseshoes
sleeps in the western mountains still.
Now and then neighing strangely he lifts himself,
he leaves behind the field of tall grass
and announces to me his preparations
for our soon-to-come victorious ultimate flight.

Tonight he is sick. He feels a sharp pain
mysteriously prodding the place where his wings
will sprout. He lies on the hay, burning white.
The moon comes in the window and lies next to him.
It is the night of the world's sickness
when all the buds burst open with a sudden cry.
Everything lies in wait. Everything—blue fire.

Herald

I come at night from the deeps of the wood:
we have a new king!
I jump over chasms with my fairy-tale spurs
to reach the gray city walls in a hurry.
Leaves whisper toward the city: Good tidings!
I avoid the many-headed funeral mound,
I run so fast across the fields that I trip on my shield.
I bump the lights above with my helmet:
He is born! He is born!

My knees give way, my forehead is on fire.
Rainbows shoot from my wake from the dew
I scatter.
From the green watchtower the guard spots me.
Silence is the fruit of the hour:
We have a king!
He does not hear me.

Rise, nobles, with your well-ordered crests,
with your martyrs and saints,
rise, you trumpeters, with your apprentices,
and you, servants, I'm bringing you news from the wood!
Last night a new king was born unto us,
a son of the forest, baby of the cuckoo!

Geological Vision

A granite bowl under the great mountain peak.
One step—abruptly, another world.

A steady and strange memory insists somewhere
in me, wafting from the green scent of junipers.

A heavy memory weighs—of other times
my blood still pulls toward and desires.

I was here once in a dream or in a life
when there was no mountain peak or pond.

I stood between vines in the equatorial heat
watched by serpents, big flowers, and monkeys.

While my body, all but body, under the humid sky
was closely watched by its own spirit

like a stranger. And the mud was still unbound,
still not taken, subdued, and remade.

Without Sundays or beginnings I hid
in silence under the leafy shields,

among roots, and vines, in equatorial heat,
loved by serpents, flowers, and monkeys.

Doubts of the Swarm

Golden, the new generation of bees is ready to swarm.
Their country is asking them to go. The mouth of the hive
is filled with the armored din. Any moment now
the adventure will begin.

Perhaps a far signal has come to delay
their departure for an hour. Or perhaps
a sudden dread will keep them, the terrible
fear of falling to the fire of the first dawn.

Words for the Unknown Girl in the Doorway

Don't refuse. You have to take on this new care:
In the doorway I have come to after crossing this valley,
you must be the guardian of my childhood. Of the childhood
I still carry in me.
It is my only good, the source, through years, seasons,
the cardinal points.
Tend it, guard the source of the spring
so that it will not dry in the wake of this time
abandoned by flower and fruit.
Take care so that the small blaze hidden
in the heart of autumn crocus won't go out.

I once had bare feet and a back burnt
by the sun's stinging nettles. I remind you
of days long gone, but do not think that I've left
my childhood behind some fence I used to jump over.
No, my childhood's with me right here, even today.
And if I were to jump over the doorway of autumn
where I have finally come, my childhood would take
the leap with me, gathered in my veins and my fists.
I only need a bit of help from you, a smile
or that blush of beauty that lights up your face.
Don't be surprised by my words. It's true,
there is some gray at the temples, and certain
oblique thoughts have been etched on my forehead.
Please blow softly over the spark still living
at the bottom of the hearth, the laughing, running spark,
the bud of light that burns
in the blood like a dying bee.

What doorway is here, truthfully? The gray door
whose name I am unwilling to pronounce?
You stop me from entering. I don't want to fade yet.
Guard me so that fulfillment won't find me too soon,
so that I won't be dead before I die—
And yet I ask myself: Girl in the doorway,
who are you? And if you are not,
where are you and how can you be?

The Red Meadow

The wet moss, the berry's black,
hold heat in balance.
Leave your sandals, goddess,
will us, Your highness!

Go barefoot in the dew!
The question lingers on
long after my rest is done:
Is this dream a real one?

The forest creatures see us:
they believe in you and me both.
With autumn's body so near now
the sun draws blood from our thought.

Red goats climb from the valley
overjoyed we borrow their strength
as they come to lay at our feet
the warmth of their summer fate.

Burning

Dear creature—will I ever find the right
silver sound, the fire-wound, the rite
of a speech equal to your endless burning?

I am the last of my seed.
A fistful of light—you, a fistful of dust.
You pomegranate, you flower to me, you celestial power,
where and when will I find the one word
that will charm you in the circle of night?

Awkward by home fires, but understood
by stones and gods,
where is that word—to lift you
like a halo from the box of time?

Where is that word—which ties
thought and deed to nothingness?
I'm giving myself to this year,
my flower, to end burning.

Vigil

My eyes are closing heavy with the long
too long prolonged difficult game.
The black comfort of sleep
would like to serve me now.

You white beauty, never setting,
you miracle that lays me waste,
it is for you I stand watch and keep awake,
nocturnal thought!

Until the hour that no clock
will strike. Behold
the playful ardors go out one by one,
how a road falls from the world.

Only I in my undisputed lateness,
servant and prince of vigils,
I sail out in search of you
on the wide wave of outgoing sleep.

On Many Roads

On many roads, on many—thought tries to find you.
Oh, that brutal end of day, that rash and sudden frost!
The flowers in my garden yearn still for those high
clearings, still call on your nameless light!

I don't know where you are sleeping now.
No song can find you. Today you are wherever you are
while I'm here. Distance has put the big chariot
of the sky between us, and the valley streams,
and the night fires on the hills—
on earth she has put passions and anemones
that do not weather well in the light of day.
A gate has been shut. Not a sign vaults the crossings.

November

Wet leaf, moss on old tombs,
drops echo in the honeycombs.

Caves and hollows meet the gaze
where the shadows come to graze.

Ancient but still ruddy fauns
moan under the boulders' dawns.

In the midday bogs
lambs fill with fog.

The hideouts are strewn
with old meanings, lost noons.

Fruit of my heart, precious bead
a tear pries open my eyelid.

Oh, I lost, what is it I lost?
The new fire, the warm ghost.

I lost the sun, I lost the moon.
Who will redeem my hollow host?

Black Thickets

Black thickets trail me, an echo.
Road moves me, pain makes me go.

Black thickets shake their shadows in me,
the hour bleeds in fog's antiphony.

Black thickets have wrapped me in a spell,
my heart's eye won't open where I fell.

Black thickets speak in the world for me:
with the noise of frost they gather fear.

Black thickets tell slow and late
about my exhausted fire.

Song for the Year 2000

The vulture circling above
will be long gone by then.

Near Sibiu, near Sibiu,
only the oaks will remain.

Will a passerby remember me
under them, to a stranger?

This is how the tale starts
should anyone announce me:

He walked about here, always returning,
a contemporary of butterflies, and of God.

Epitaph

The road is not easily found here.
There is no one to guide you.
Only very late, a brief instant,
soon-to-be-forgotten, reveals
the unexpected steps.

Then like a leaf you fall. You pull
the dirt over your eyes
like a heavy lid.
The holy mothers—
the myriad lights,
the mothers in the earth,
receive your words.
And again they feed you.

The Dog from Pompeii

I saw this Roman dog in Pompeii.
This is the way the fates wanted him—
a mold preserved in the material of death—
neither rain nor time can rot him.

He'd gone out to escape the cloud at the door,
the night of fire fallen from the mountain.
But this dog, turning briefly in place,
was caught grinning and biting the ashes instead.

I see you, God—lead, ash, and cloud—
coming to meet me at my door,
crushing in from the sky, from the hot mountain.

I will escape through this gate. And then
I will bite in You the ash of this world.
I will preserve my earthly print in You.

BLAGA CHRONOLOGY

1895 May 9: Lucian Blaga is born in Lancrăm, southern Transylvania, at that time part of the Austro-Hungarian monarchy. He is the ninth and last child of Isidor Blaga, a Romanian Orthodox priest, and Ana Moga, granddaughter of distinguished Orthodox bishop.

1902-06 Attends German primary school in nearby Sebeş.

1906-08 Secondary education at the Andrei Şaguna Gymnasium in Braşov.

1908 His father dies, and Blaga is withdrawn temporarily from school because of financial difficulties. Reads Goethe's *Faust* at home, his "most important literary discover."

1909-10 Family moves to Sebeş, where Blaga attends high school. Early readings in German and Hindu philosophy. First poems published in *Tribuna* [The tribune] and *Românul* [The Romanian] from Arad.

1914 Publishes his first theoretical essay, "Reflections on Bergsonian Intuition," in *Românul*. Enrolls at the Sibiu Orthodox Seminary mainly to avoid induction into the Hapsburg army.

1916 First trip to Vienna, where he discovers the Expressionist movement and meets his future wife, Cornelia Brediceanu, daughter of a prominent politician from the Banat area and sister to composer Tiberiu Brediceanu.

1917 Obtains theology dress. Studies philosophy and biology at the University of Vienna. Begins *Poems of Light*, many inspired by his love for Cornelia Brediceanu.

1918 Shortly after the signing of the Armistice, the provinces of Banat, Crişana, Transylvania, Bessarabia, and Bucovina are united with Romania. President Woodrow Wilson welcomes the first Romanian ambassador to America.

1919 *Poemele luminii* [Poems of light] appears in the Cernăuţi magazine *Glasul Bucovinei* [The voice of Bucovina] and in book form. Publication of *Pietre pentru templul meu* [Stones for my temple], a collection of philosophical reflections. Both are reviewed enthusiastically by major critics (Sextil Puşcariu, Nicolae Iorga, Ovid Densusianu) and are awarded the Adamachi Prize of the Romanian Academy.

1920 Receives Ph.D. from Vienna. Dissertation: *Kultur und erkenntnis* [Culture and cognition] (translated into Romanian in 1922). Marries Cornelia Brediceanu.

1921 Publication of *Paşii profetului* [The footprints of the prophet] and first play, *Zamolxe* [Zamolxes]. Joins the Romanian Writers' Society and cofounds *Gândirea* [Thought], a major Transylvanian review in which he publishes many poems and essays. (In 1942, Blaga dissociated himself from the "strictly orthodox" mysticism cultivated in *Gândirea*.)

1923 Another play, *Tulburarea apelor* [Stirred waters], is published.

1924 Stays in Lugoj (Banat) with his wife's family. *În marea trecere* [In the great passing], a collection of new poems, and *Filozofia stilului* [The philosophy of style] are published.

1925 Two new plays, *Daria* [Daria] and *Fapta* [The deed], appear, followed by two collections of essays, *Fenomenul originar* [The original phenomenon] and *Feţele unui veac* [Faces of an age].

1926 Appointed press secretary to the Romanian royal legation in Warsaw.

1927 Transferred to the Romanian legation in Prague. Publication of major play, *Meşterul Manole* [Master Manole].

1928 Reassigned to the Romanian legation in Bern, where he works with Nicolae Titulescu. G. Călinescu publishes the first important retrospective essay on Blaga's poetry in *Gândirea*. A younger generation of critics (Tudor Vianu, Perpessicius, Vladimir Streinu, Octav Şuluţiu, Şerban Cioculescu) establishes Blaga's place as a major national poet.

1929 Publishes his fifth collection of poems, *Lauda somnului* [In praise of sleep]. *Meşterul Manole* is staged in Bucharest and Bern.

1930 Blaga's daughter, Anan Dorica (Dorli), born in Bern. "Daimon," a philosophical essay, and *Cruciada copiilor* [The children's crusade], a play, are published. *Lauda somnului* receives the Romanian Writers' Poetry Award.

1931 Publication of *Eonul dogmatic* [The dogmatic age], the first part of Blaga's *Trilogy of Knowledge*.

1932 Blaga is appointed press attaché to the Romanian embassy in Vienna.

1933 Publication if *La cumpăna apelor* [On the great water divide], a collection of poems, and *Cunoaşterea luciferică* [Luciferic cognition], the second volume of Blaga's trilogy on knowledge.

1934 *Cenzura transcendentală* [Transcendental censorship] completes Blaga's first philosophic trilogy. *Avram Iancu*, a historical play, is also published. *Gândirea* devotes a special issue to Blaga, with contributions from Tudor Vianu, Emil Cioran, Dragoş Protopopescu, and others.

1935 Awarded the prestigious C. Hamangiu Prize of the Romanian Academy for "his dramatic and poetic work of the past six years."

1936 Publication of the first two parts of Blaga's *Trilogy of Culture: Orizont şi stil* [Horizon and style] and *Spaţiul mioritic* [Mioritic space]. Blaga is elected an active member of the Romanian Academy.

1937 Blaga delivers his acceptance speech to the academy, "Eulogy of the Romanian Village." *Geneza metaforei şi sensul culturii* [The emergence of metaphor and the meaning of culture], the third part of his trilogy on the philosophy of culture, is published.

1938 Appointed Romania's ambassador to Lisbon, Portugal. *La curţile dorului* [At the court of yearning] is published. In *Revista fundaţiilor regale* [Lucian Blaga and the meaning of culture], Mircea Eliade highlights the originality of Blaga's philosophy. (Thirty years later he will rank Blaga above Sartre and Gabriel Marcel and deplore the lack of adequate translations of his work in the West.)

1939 Blaga gives up his diplomatic career and returns to Romania. Teaches cultural philosophy at the university of Cluj. *Artă și valoare* [Art and value], the first part of the *Trilogy of Values*, appears.

1940 Following the temporary occupation of northern Transylvania by Horthy's Hungarian army, Blaga seeks refuge in Sibiu. Publishes *Diferențialele divine* [Divine differentials], the first part of a never-completed "cosmological trilogy."

1941 *Despre Gândirea magică* [On magic thinking] appears.

1942 Publication of Blaga's *Collected Plays* (2 vols. [Sibiu: Dacia Traiana Press]) and *Poems* in definitive edition (Bucharest: Royal Foundation for Literature and Art). *Religie și spirit* [Religion and spirit] and *Știință si creație* [Science and creation], the last two parts of Blaga's trilogy on values, appear. Quits *Gândirea* because of its pro-fascist orientation.

1943 Edits *Saeculum* in Sibiu (February 1943-April 1944), a philosophic and cultural review that carries several of his essays. *Nebănuitele trepte* [The unsuspected stair] appears, followed by a one-volume edition of Blaga's *Trilogy of Knowledge* (Bucharest: Royal Foundation of Literature and Art).

1944 Publication of *Arca lui Noe* [Noah's ark], a play. The *Trilogy of Culture* is published in a single volume.

1945 Publication of *Discobolul* [Discobolus], a collection of aphorisms. After the Soviet imposition of a Communist government in Romania, Lucrețiu Pătrășcanu, the Party ideologue, attacks Blaga's "eclectic and agnostic" work in "Lucian Blaga and the Crisis of Romanian Philosophy."

1946 The *Trilogy of Values* is published in a single volume. *Horizon and Style* appears in Italy (trans. Mircea Popescu and Eugenio Coseriu). Nestor Ignat, earlier a student of Blaga, publishes a virulent attack on his former teacher ("Casul Blaga" [The Blaga case]), calling on socialist history to "censor and bury Mr. Blaga without remorse."

1947-48 Blaga's lectures *Despre conştiinţa filozofică* [On philosophic consciousness] and the second part of his projected "cosmological trilogy," *Aspecte antropologie* [Anthropological aspects], appear in mimeographed form.

1948 Blaga excluded from the reorganized Academy of Communist Romania.

1949 Blaga's chair of cultural philosophy closed down by the Communist authorities. In the following years, Blaga holds marginal, badly remunerated positions as a university librarian or researcher. His poetic and philosophic works are banned until shortly before his death.

1950 Works on a historical survey, *Romanian Philosophic Thought in Transylvania during the Eighteenth Century*, published posthumously. New attacks in the part press on Blaga's "morbid, nihilistic, misty poetry," inspired by the "decadent ideology" of the West.

1955 Blaga's acclaimed translation of Goethe's *Faust* appears. For almost a decade Blaga is allowed to publish only translations of other works into Romanian.

1956 A high party delegation visits Blaga in Cluj, demanding that he publicly abjure his "irrationalist" philosophy and embrace the "new humanism." Blaga refuses, arguing that he cannot unwrite his previous philosophy, nor has be the energy to create a new system.

1957 Blaga translations entitled *Din lirica universală* [From world poetry] appear.

1958 A two-volume edition of Lessing's works appears in Blaga's translation.

1959 Mihai Beniuc, former secretary of the Writers' Union, publishes new attacks on Blaga in an article and a thinly disguised novel, *Pe muche de cuţit* [On a knife's edge].

1960 Blaga contributes a few semipropagandistic articles and new poems to several literary magazines.

1961 Dies May 6. Buried modestly in his native village of Lancrăm.

1962 Blaga's poems republished after fifteen years of interdiction. George Ivaşcu, the editor, includes a few previously uncollected poems from literary magazines.

1968 Publication of *Poemele luminii. Mirabila sămînţă* [Poems of light. The wondrous seed] in 2 vols., containing new cycles of poems written after the war. Blaga's early philosophic reflections are republished in *Zări şi etape* [Horizon and stages] (ed. Dorli Blaga).

1969 The *Trilogy of Culture* reissued (ed. Sorin Mărculescu and D. Ghişe).

1970 A selection of Blaga's translations from English poetry published.

1974 The first two volumes of Blaga's complete works (*Poems*, ed. Dorli Blaga, preface by Şerban Cioculescu) are published by Minerva Press, Bucharest. This edition, still incomplete, also includes vol. 3, *Translations* (1975); vols. 4-5, *Plays* (1977); vol. 6, *Autobiographical Prose* (1979); vol. 7, *Essays* (1980); vol. 8, *Trilogy of Knowledge* (1983); vol. 9, *Trilogy of Culture* (1985); and vol. 10, *Trilogy of Values* (1987).

1975 First book-length translations of Blaga's poems into English: *Poemele luminii/Poems of light*, trans. Don Eulert, Ştefan Avădanei, and Mihail Bogdan, preface by Constantin Ciopraga (Bucharest: Minerva, 351 pp.); *În marea trecere/The Great Transition*, trans. Roy MacGregor-Hastie (Bucharest: Eminescu, 200 pp.).

1982 George Gană begins an alternative edition of Blaga's works with vol. 1, *Poezii antume* [Previously published poems]. Extensive critical notes and variants follow the carefully edited texts. Two more volumes have appeared: vol. 2, *Poezii postume* [Posthumous poems] (1984], and vol. 3, *Teatru* [Plays] (1986).

1989 Andrei Codrescu translates all of Blaga's poetry published before 1946, with an introduction, *At the Court of Yearning*, followed by an Afterword by Marcel Cornis-Pop (University of Ohio Press, 1989).

2018 Black Widow Press publishes *In Praise of Sleep*, poems by Lucian Blaga, translated with revised, with an introduction by Andrei Codrescu.

INDEX OF TITLES

BLACK WIDOW PRESS
POETRY IN TRANSLATION

Through Naked Branches:
Selected Poems of Tarjei Vesaas
Translated by Roger Greenwald

I Have Invented Nothing:
Selected Poems
by Jean-Pierre Rosnay.
Translated by J. Kates

Fables of Town & Country
by Pierre Coran.
Translated by Norman R. Shapiro.
Illustrated by Olga Pastuchiv.

Earthlight (Clair de terre): Poems
by André Breton;
Translated by Bill Zavatsky and
Zack Rogow.

The Gentle Genius of Cecile Perin:
Selected Poems (1906-1956)
Translated by Norman R. Shapiro

Boris Vian Invents Boris Vian:
A Boris Vian reader
Edited and Translated by Julia
Older. Preface by Patrick Vian

Forbidden Pleasures:
New Selected Poems [1924-1949]
by Luis Cernuda. Translated by
Stephen Kessler

Fables In a Modern Key (Fables
Dans L'Air Du Temps) by Pierre
Coran. Translated by Norman
R. Shapiro. Illustrated by Olga
Pastuchiv
Exile Is My Trade: A Habib Ten-
gour Reader
Translated by Pierre Joris

Present Tense of The World:
Poems 2000-2009
by Amina Said
Translated by Marilyn Hacker

Endure: Poems by Bei Dao
Translated by Clayton
Eshleman and Lucas Klein
Curdled Skulls:
Poems of Bernard Bador
Co-translated and edited by Clay-
ton Eshleman

Pierre Reverdy: Poems Early to Late
by Pierre Reverdy
Translated by Mary Ann Caws
and Patricia Terry

Selected Prose and Poetry
of Jules Supervielle.
Translated by Nancy Kline, Patri-
ca Terry and Kathleen Micklow.

Poems of Consummation
by Vicente Aleixandre
Translated by Stephen Kessler

A Life of Poems, Poems of a Life
by Anna de Noailles
Translated by Norman R. Shapiro

Furor & Mystery and Other Poems
by Rene Char.
Translated by Mary Ann Caws
and Nancy Kline

The Big Game (Le grand jeu)
by Benjamin Péret.
Translated by Marilyn Kallet

Essential Poems & Prose of
Jules Laforgue
Translated by Patricia Terry.
Preversities:
A Jacques Prevert Sampler
Translated by Norman R. Shapiro.

La Fontaine's Bawdy
by Jean de la Fontaine
Translated by Norman R. Shapiro
Illustrated by David Schorr

BLACK WIDOW PRESS
MODERN POETS AND BIOGRAPHY

ABC of Translation
by Willis Barnstone

The Secret Brain:
Selected Poems 1995-2012
by Dave Brinks

Caveat Onus:
The Complete Poem Cycle
by Dave Brinks

Crusader Woman
by Ruxandra Cesereanu.
Translated by Cesereanu
and Adam Sorkin

Forgiven Submarine
by Andrei Codrescu
and Ruxandra Cesereanu.
Translated by Andrei Codrescu

Anticline
by Clayton Eshleman

Archaic Design
by Clayton Eshleman

Alchemist with One Eye on Fire
by Clayton Eshleman

The Price of Experience
by Clayton Eshleman

The Essential Poetry (1960 to 2015)
by Clayton Eshleman

Grindstone of Rapport:
A Clayton Eshleman Reader

Penetralia by Clayton Eshleman

Clayton Eshleman:
The Whole Art
Edited by Stuart Kendall

Barzakh (Poems 2000-2012)
by Pierre Joris
Packing Light: New & Selected
Poems by Marilyn Kallet
How Our Bodies Learned
by Marilyn Kallet

The Love That Moves Me
by Marilyn Kallet

The Hexagon
by Robert Kelly

Fire Exit
by Robert Kelly

Garage Elegies
by Stephen Kessler

Memory Wing
by Bill Lavender

from stone this running
by Heller Levinson

Wrack Lariat
by Heller Levinson

LinguaQuake
by Heller Levinson

tenebraed
by Heller Levinson

Dada Budapest
by John Olson

Backscatter
by John Olson

Larynx Galaxy
by John Olson

City Without People:
The Katrina Poems
by Niyi Osundare

An American Unconscious
by Mebane Robertson
Signal from Draco:
New & Selected Poems
by Mebane Robertson

Barbaric Vast & Wild:
An Assemblage of Outside
& Subterranean Poetry
from Origins to Present
Edited by Jerome Rothenberg
and John Bloomberg-Rissman

Concealments and Caprichos
by Jerome Rothenberg

Eye of Witness:
A Jerome Rothenberg Reader
Edited by Heribeto Yepez
and Jerome Rothenberg

Soraya
by Anis Shivani

Exile Is My Trade:
A Habib Tengour Reader
Translated by Pierre Joris

Fractal Song
by Jerry W. Ward, Jr.

BIOGRAPHY

Revolution of the Mind:
The Life of Andre Breton
by Mark Polizzotti